About the Author

Natasha Fay overcame a life of abuse and exploitation in her childhood through strength and determination. She is a true survivor.
She lives in Tasmania, has a successful career and a daughter whom she adores. In her spare time, she enjoys dancing and the company of good friends. *Nobody's Child* is her brilliant debut novel.

*My precious daughter Madelyn, it is you who I live for.
To all the children of the world, may they live in safety.*

Natasha Fay

NOBODY'S CHILD

Copyright © Natasha Fay (2016)

The right of Natasha Fay to be identified as author of this work has been asserted by her in accordance with section 77 and 78 of the Copyright, Designs and Patents Act 1988.

All rights reserved. No part of this publication may be reproduced, stored in a retrieval system, or transmitted in any form or by any means, electronic, mechanical, photocopying, recording, or otherwise, without the prior permission of the publishers.

Any person who commits any unauthorized act in relation to this publication may be liable to criminal prosecution and civil claims for damages.

A CIP catalogue record for this title is available.

ISBN 978-0-6484085-1-2 (Paperback)
ISBN 978-0-6484085-0-5 (E-Book)

First Published (2016) Austin Macauley Publishers
Second Edition (2018) Natasha Fay

Thanks to Moira for her help and collaboration on this project and her steadfast belief in me and the importance of my story being told. Thanks to Tim for his contribution and support.

Thank you to Sharon and Robin and also to my good friend Dion, who's support, and encouragement has been beyond anything expected.

"When you have never had anything throughout life, it's the smallest of things that make the biggest difference."

From the Author

Abuse happens in many forms and in this book I share with you the abuse I have suffered and the resultant effects on my life both growing up and as an adult. I consider this abuse to be mainly of a sexual nature although as an innocent child I could not name it as such. I just felt different, scared, dirty and unworthy and unable to allow myself to get close to anyone. I still grapple with these types of feelings now. As I have grown I have also come to realise that many other forms of abuse were inflicted upon me as well, from the psychological torture of the men who treated me inappropriately to the emotional abuse of my family, particularly through the complicity of my mother – whom it transpires was an earlier victim herself. It is prudent to point out from the outset, that whilst the facts of my story are true and also backed up by official documentation, it is not a timeline diary as such. I have been true to dates as much as possible but far more importantly it is a memory account of my life and the events therein. Much of the reason for my continuing existence today, is my firm belief that whatever my dilemmas, there are people worse off than me. This philosophy has stood me in good stead up to now, but I realise that it falls short of the ultimate mark.

It is time for a survivor to stand up and scream aloud to the world that the ramifications of abuse can be overcome and the cycle broken. I have wanted to tell my story for many years but now it is the right time in my life to do it – I want to move on. I want to leave behind the shocking feeling of loneliness which I have been scared to share with others because I have felt unworthy of their time and attention. Now I want to let other people in and for them to know the real me. I have always been a loyal friend to others but ever reluctant to accept their support or help because it's something I actually never had in my life and in this context it has been hard to trust good and positive things when they do happen, because they are strangers to me. I have had great difficulty with my friendships and relationships. I always tried too hard and became a people-pleaser to get approval because I had known no other way. Naturally this has applied to the men in my life as well, as love equating to pleasing them in a sexual context was drummed into me as a child.

So consequently I have done things I am not proud of but a great change has occurred in my life recently which allows for a new outlook and a new way of living and being. I am slowly learning to let other people in. This is why now is the right time to tell my story to the world, both for myself and for others who have suffered as I have. I have come to accept that I was a victim of the cruelty and depravity of others, and that as a victim I AM NOT TO BLAME. What a defining and life-changing revelation! I have accepted that my childhood was not normal, not okay, not right and not fair. I have apportioned blame where it is due and used the channels of the police and courts both in Tasmania and Victoria to redress my abuse and demand that I be heard.

Possibly the most cathartic experience of all was facing my own mother down and demanding that she take responsibility for the horrors of my childhood, letting her know that as a mother she was an abuser of sorts herself and had not protected or cared for me. Why did it take all those years until I was a mother myself in my forties, to do this? Perhaps I needed the strength of the years to realise that I would again be rejected by her! So it is with an ever growing sense of self – belief that I share my story with you, not for pity, but for your outrage that in modern Australia so many little children have suffered and are suffering right now like I did. There is never any excuse for a child to suffer! Let us band together and be vigilant so that they all make the transition from victim to survivor, as I have done.

Natasha Fay.

Chapter One

The Fear Begins

My entry into the world was a difficult one. I have been told over and again by my mother that she did not want to be pregnant with me, and that she threw herself deliberately down a flight of stairs in order to self-abort. Sadly for her, this did not succeed. It was not her first pregnancy but obviously the one that she did not want. I was always told that I was unwanted and the mistaken result of an affair and as our lives together showed she certainly never changed that view. I was born with an extra tailbone and other physically unusual traits and a doctor once told me that I may have been a possible Siamese twin. At any rate the thought that I may have actually been one of two has given me so much comfort over the years, one because it gave me strength to carry on 'for us both' and two because another child was spared the life I have had.

I had no name given to me at or around the time of my birth in Hobart in 1973.

This obviously worried a friend of my mother who was looking after me and so she gave me my name – Natasha Fay. (Fay was her middle name.) The man my mum was married to at the time was not my father, but my step-father (according to mum) and although I have since been told my real father's name by mum, I was then far too young to seek him out.

I guess that before my own personal abuse began the cycle of abuse was already well ingrained into my family and somewhat accepted because no-one seemed to make a song and dance about it. My mother was practically absent from my life from the day I was born, so she obviously harboured no great concerns for my safety or my well-being. And it transpired that mum had actually been raped as a teenager and harboured some very dark family secrets as well...What a hell on earth for a girl baby to be injected into, what hope that her childhood would be wholesome and secure?

There was none.

My most serious sexual abuse was not perpetrated by blood relatives, and I am greatly relieved about that, however luck may have played a role, as when I was fifteen a close male relative demanded that I remove my top for "a feel." Supposedly this was because I neither had, nor wanted a boyfriend and he was concerned I might turn gay! By this stage of years of conditioning at the hands of my abusers, I felt I had no choice – hating every second of the experience (as usual.) Thank God I didn't often see him alone... At this juncture I would like to share with you that I had two sisters, a brother and a half-brother (my stepfather's son.) It may sound incredible to those who live outside the curtain of sexual abuse but in our warped family we did not share our experiences or the horrors of abuse. We were trained to secrecy and knew no other way of life. Obviously we were all extremely damaged as individuals, isolated and inhibited socially and emotionally and life was far from normal. But to us this was what normal was. I am certainly not at liberty to tell my sisters' stories but suffice to say that it was many years after leaving that hideous environment that we shared a walk together and had 'that' discussion. They have indicated to me that they would rather I did not write this book and I empathise with their feelings, but the subject matter is bigger than all of us and I am of the conviction that it must be told in order to help myself, and others. So it is fair to say that as siblings we were never close enough to share intimacies – or anything much at all really. What encouragement did we have to trust or to foster warm relationships in our own home or to develop a sense of security, of place, of self? For me anyway there was none and this is the best way I can explain the coldness, the ambivalence we all felt towards each other and our lack of sharing or communication.

It was a lonely world inside the houses in which we lived, except for the constant dark companions of fear and shame.

If as children we had no sense of our place in the world, then how could we possibly defend it?

How could we have complained of a situation which was all that we had ever known and how could we not have been monumentally affected and damaged by this situation?

Anyway, back to the little baby girl who was named by another – not her mother. When I was taken home from hospital my mother showed her contempt of me through absence and neglect. It was not unusual for me to go hungry and unchanged and so I spent much time being cared for by the woman who had given me an identity. Sadly for me, mum left her then husband (my first step-father) whilst I was a baby and moved us all to

Victoria to pursue numerous other romantic relationships. This was the time that as little more than a babe, my life took another of its ugly turns.

My first clear and horrific memory of sexual abuse occurred when I was about five years old. There is no reason to suppose given the circumstances, that this was my first sexual experience with this particular man but it is the first that I remember so vividly.

I don't know where my mother was, but I do remember the excitement my brother and I felt at being taken to the Traralgon Show in Victoria with a friend of the family and his wife. It was a beautiful, clear evening with the smell of animals, fast foods, and the happy noise of families milling around everywhere enjoying themselves. I was so very happy to be there. During all the excitement and festivity my brother somehow wandered away from us and the family friend decided that he would take me away from the area to search for my brother, leaving his wife behind. The man kept a tight grip on my hand, but I became instinctively terrified of him and very upset and managed to break away. I had a strong feeling that he had done "bad things" to me before. I ran over to a side-show game near the oval, crying and hoping that the lady there would help me to be safe. The horrible man caught up to me and made some excuse to the side-show lady and dragged me away. I couldn't explain to the lady why I was crying, upset and scared and so what could I do? *Nothing!* A five-year-old has no power and little ability to articulate in a situation such as that. I was dragged by him into the toilets, placed on the toilet seat so that my little legs were apart and brutalised with his fingers through my screams of pain and shock. Once satisfied with his abuse the family friend pulled up my pants and roughly escorted me outside.

I had never known such pain! I couldn't walk properly and my screams came from somewhere within the depths of my little soul. Nobody approached to see if I was alright in that sea of people, and I guess he would have made up another excuse anyway.

One of my most enraging memories of that evening (looking back) was that this vile sexual pervert tried to give me a fifty dollar note to shut me up so that it would not come to light that he had ravaged my hymen, stolen my innocence and caused me irrevocable harm.

When we were reunited with his wife (who had found my brother) I recall her being told that I was crying because I too, had become lost. I remember nothing at all else of the show or the journey back to their home until I was told to have my bath.

I guess now that I was in severe, debilitating shock.

Whilst in the bath I remember seeing blood everywhere and I didn't understand why – but I was the most frightened little girl in the world at that moment. I sat in my bath of bloody water and cried until no more tears would come. Would that this were to be the end to this story... I badly wanted the security and safety of sleeping in the room with my brother that night, but of course my abuser made me sleep in the lounge room so that he could have easy access to me during the hours of darkness.

I remember the relief I felt when his wife called out to him and he eventually returned to the marital bedroom. My memories are as clear as if it had all happened only yesterday, God help me.

To give a context to what happened next, I will relate a little story involving my mother which occurred when I was around this same age. She had visited a fast food shop and we children were waiting in the car for her return, as instructed. I saw a beautiful Samoyed dog on the footpath and with a child's enthusiasm jumped out of the car to pat him. The dog attacked me and I lost a chunk out of my right cheek. Such a commotion in the street!

I was taken to hospital and my treating doctor called the police, believing that my wound was similar to a stab wound and surmising that my mother had tried to kill me. That was not the case – but what was it about my condition, or my mother, which led him to believe this?

The crux of the story is that my mother saw an opportunity in the situation and on 'my behalf' sued the dog!

I became the first person in Australia to sue a bloody dog. Obviously it turned out well because the poor creature was destroyed and compensation was held in trust for me until I turned eighteen. How confusing, to feel the suspicion of the hospital staff towards my mother, to need her comfort so badly which was not forthcoming and to feel the guilt of the dog's death (although it scared me too.)

The day after my horrific sexual abuse, my brother and I were taken home, whereupon I hid my bloody pants in the laundry amongst other clothes through fear and shame. My mother did take me to a doctor when they were discovered, although I told her I only had suffered a bleeding nose. Either this doctor only examined my nose or decided to avoid the then 'taboo' subject of child sexual abuse – I will never know. But I know as an adult that my mother (and he) should have read the signs shining like a beacon at them and *done something*. I was left with a feeling that what had happened to me was normal, happened to other children and in the eyes of adults was perfectly okay. As a five-year-old I could not articulate well my dilemma, but they were not listening anyway. My relationship with my mother was an extremely destructive one for me. Her emotional, psychological and verbal abuse peppered my childhood from a young age and the one certainty in life that I could depend on even then, was that she neither wanted me nor loved me. I was extremely neglected physically, as all my medical records suggest, and I do know that she was complicit in some periods of my sexual abuse and exploitation at the hands of one of her partners.

Childhood Medical Records

▬▬▬▬▬▬▬
M.B., B.S., F.R.A.C.G.P., D.Obst.R.C.O.G.

MORWELL COMMUNITY HEALTH CENTRE
P.O. Box 000, MORWELL 3840
Telephone: (051) 34 2011
Private: (051) 34 2315

Our Ref. GBP:mmo S/0029B
Your Ref. KR/BR-92H139625

30th November, 1992.

▬▬▬▬▬▬▬
Legal Aid Commission of Tasmania
GPO Box 9090
HOBART 7001

Dear Sir,

re : Natasha ▬▬▬▬▬▬▬
d.o.b. 11/11/73

I reply to your letters of 14th and 29th October, 1992, and not allegation of sexual assault during the Traralgon Show in 1978 or 1979

The consultations recorded in Natasha's notes are as follows :-

11/5/77	-	Removal of Sutures.
12/7/78	-	Throat Infection.
24/10/78	-	Tonsillitis.
15/11/78	-	Chicken Pox.
20/11/78	-	Infected Sores on Legs.
9/2/79	-	Gastroenteritis.
8/7/80	-	Review of Old Scar Right Cheek.
11/9/80	-	Respiratory Infection.
1/6/81	-	Referred for Vision Test.
22/6/81	-	U.R.T.I.
9/7/81	-	U.R.T.I.
14/7/81	-	U.R.T.I.
24/9/81	-	Pimples on Face.
31/10/81	-	Tonsillitis.
21/2/83	-	"2 Boils on Bottom" - examination normal.
6/3/83	-	Throat Infection.

Two other visits on 14/11/79 and 19/5/80 were for ear pierce performed by the Clinic Sister.

A referral to the eye specialist was written on 7/6/82.

I confirm again that there is no record of Natasha being examined this Centre since 1977 in relation to alleged sexual assault.

I confirm that the account for my report of 10/6/92 has been paid.

Yours faithfully,

▬▬▬▬▬▬▬

Why I have no idea, except to surmise that it was because she had been a victim herself of sexual abuse and its negative consequence of engaging in negative, warped relationships (at the expense of her poor children) – an unhappy and destructive cycle for us all.

I was not asked to be born, indeed she tried to prevent my birth as I explained at the start but since I had come into the world, why had she not cared about me? More on this later, but I include it now to show that my abuse was not only sexual in nature but that my 'protector, my rock' – *my MOTHER!* – ensured that it extended far beyond the sexual to providing a hell on earth for me which I had no way of understanding.

I still don't.

As a combination of the treatment I received at the hands of my mother and the hideously regular sexual abuse which became a normal part of my life, I was a quiet little girl.

From as far back as I can remember I believed totally that I was completely worthless and that whatever I did was wrong, just not good enough. I had no confidence and therefore no voice so that I would find myself doing activities at school which I did not like simply because another child thought I should. I became a ridiculous people pleaser, which is still a feature of my adult life in some ways. I always did what I was told and took pride in my schoolwork and getting things 'right'. Possibly due to the fact that we moved around so much, not one teacher picked up on any signs that my life was not normal but I do remember that I made some macabre drawings in class, which I believe should have rung some bells – especially the detailed one of a penis and its accoutrements in grade two.

I remember that my mother was shown this drawing but all that happened (so far as I know) was that it disappeared and was not referred to again. I lived with a constant sense of shame and fear. It is difficult to describe this adequately, but I had a sense that I was different to the other little girls around me who seemed so carefree and spontaneous.

I always felt a burden weighing on me, of adult secrets and stealth which I could not begin to comprehend but caused me great stress and uncertainty.

On the one hand, what kept happening to me at the hands of men 'must' have been normal, (I knew no different) but on the other hand it isolated me from the world and most importantly, from myself.

A SAD PLEA TO MY MUMMY

Who is there to hold me?

You do not love me mum.

I cannot share my tears with you, so now I've just gone numb.

Maybe I'll try harder at my schoolwork and my chores,

And you might stop the terrors going on behind closed doors.

But you already know of these, so you must think it's fine – That I wish that I were dead, and I am not yet nine.

Mummy I am scared of them, the men with greasy hands. Please help me! I am alone in this, too small to take a stand.

I am just a little girl; I need to be protected!
Loved and hugged and made feel safe, not by you, rejected.
One day I'll grow up I know, and have the strength to run. I just pray that in your shoes, I'll be a better mum.

My mother had a partner who lived with us (a stepdad) of whom I was very intimidated and with good reason. His sexual exploitation of me as a young girl was constant and unrelenting. Looking back, I do not know how I coped in this situation except to say that he was an authority figure in my life and a figure of 'trust'. What I found to be especially confusing was that mum was there in the house with us and indeed would often instigate these sessions. She would call me into the bedroom she shared with him and encourage me to scratch her partner's back (as he found this pleasurable, obviously) and then mum would leave the room so he could really begin his abuse. I often felt in some weird kind of dream state with him and had no choice but think his behaviour was normal – otherwise why would my mother make it all happen? Confusion abounded in my mind but this was all just a way of life, the way of my life as a child anyway. It is interesting that this particular man was not acquainted with the so-called 'family friend' who was my other main abuser, which only served to help make me believe that what they were doing to me was normal behaviour for a man with a little girl and an opportunity. At one time my whole family were staying with this friend and his wife, possibly because we had nowhere to live at that particular time.

By now you will not be surprised that this happened after my dreadful experience the day of the Traralgon Show – my mother had no qualms about placing me and my siblings in that setting once again. In a terrible psychological replay of that night of horror which I had previously endured I was made yet again to sleep on the couch in the lounge room. My abuser once again approached me during the night, this time with a sneakier ploy. He suggested that I come to sleep in his bed saying that it would be so much more comfortable there for me. I literally jumped at the chance as I knew his wife lay in that bed and that therefore, this time I would be safe from his abuse. Oh, the innocence of a child... My abuser positioned his body in the centre of the bed and I spent an agonizing several hours being touched in any way he wanted. How strange it is that in a house containing more than half a dozen people in cramped quarters that such an outrage could be committed, even to the point that a grown woman was asleep in the very same bed! Although this sounds unusual, perhaps even difficult to believe, it is not an unusual situation in terms of child sexual abuse and exploitation. Since I know this from personal experience, as a mother now myself I do not condone sleep overs for my child, no matter how many people are present in the house. Evil has a way of leaping obstacles.

Chapter Two

Not All Bad – Some Happy Days

I guess by now that you understand my early life growing up was scary, confusing and in a word dreadful. It certainly was, and my sexual abuse continued in a steady manner for years to come until I was almost thirteen years old. I sometimes wonder if the men who treated me in the ways they did were primarily paedophiles, preying only on younger children or whether that because I was now a teenager the threat of unwanted pregnancy (and therefore discovery) was what made them cease their behaviour. Perhaps it was because mum had moved on from them. Either way, I was cast aside and rejected once again for being me – even by the most evil people in my life.

My childhood had some joy in it as well, which I take great pride in recounting. I think I was saved by the happy times, however fleeting they were. In a world where institutions are being brought to account for various forms of child abuse such as I have suffered, there was one institution run by child protection called Swan House in Sale, Victoria, which was absolutely wonderful in every way.

Very sadly, Swan House no longer exists but my memories are crystal clear. I have records which show that I stayed at Swan House on five separate occasions with various combinations of my siblings. My memories of this place are the happiest of my life and I hoped that I could live there forever in safety and happiness and security, with all the caring staff and fun activities.

Swan House was entered through huge gates at the end of a long drive with rows of orange trees on either side. From the left of the entrance was a large dining room and behind this was the kitchen, with a bench divider separating the two areas. When meals were being served this divider was opened. From the dining room sliding doors led out to the veranda. From the entrance to the right there was a television room and then a long hallway, half way along which were the baby bathrooms and then the boys' and girls' bathrooms and showers. At the end of the hallway were the children's bedrooms which were massive and contained many beds and several cots. Behind the building there was a huge sandpit, and swings and a myriad of toys – all the things children love. It was a place where there were routines and rules, but no abuse whatsoever and no emotional torture. I wanted those happy times to stay with me forever and feel very sad that I could not spend the rest of my growing years permanently with Swan House as my home.

My dreams and my happiness were shattered when my mother arrived to take me away, particularly on the day of our swimming carnival when she would not wait for me to have my turn in the beautiful pool. How sad it was that I was heartbroken to be reunited with my mother you may think, but to be plucked from security and safety into her world again was unthinkable and a total disaster for me.

I believe I developed my adult love of the theatre thanks to being at Swan House as we girls in residence at one time were taken on a special outing to see a live performance of 'Beauty and the Beast' and it was spectacular.

This experience and the pleasure it gave me lives with me to this day.

Another amazing experience and precious memory I have is that of Christmas at Swan House. A group of people on motorbikes arrived with Santa, who gave presents to us all. (I now know that this institution catered for a maximum of sixteen children at any one given time, so we were not a huge crowd.) I was given a little blue teddy bear which I instantly called 'Bluey' and I loved that teddy with my whole heart. He became my friend and my one support and the most precious thing in my whole, miserable life.

How I loved him! That was by far the best Christmas I had ever had, and even now as an adult I cherish the memory.

Being in residence and in the care of Swan House was without doubt, the best part of my childhood.

Some certain smells in my life even now transport me back to my happy times there. The smell of changing rooms in the gyms or swimming pools I sometimes attend remind me of shower time and the smell of toast sometimes takes me back to breakfast time in the large dining room full of happy, noisy children. What a perfect example of a wonderful institution run by worthy, caring and responsible people! Thank you Swan House, with all my heart.

In this chapter I would like to include some factual information about the history of Swan House, as there are no pictorial records available. The Child Protection Society was founded at a meeting at Government House on 21st March 1896 as the Victorian Society for the Prevention of Cruelty to Children (VSPCC). Its aims were to protect children from cruelty and neglect, to advance the claims of neglected, abandoned and orphaned children to the general public, to co-operate with existing societies for this service and to enforce the laws for the protection of neglected children and juvenile offenders.

From the 1920's to 1980's the society provided services across metropolitan Melbourne and rural Victoria governed by a central and a range of rural committees.

The work of the society was to investigate reports of child abuse and neglect and also provide temporary emergency care in small residential units.

These units were based in Fitzroy, Heidelberg, Sale and Hamilton. In 1971 the society changed its name to the Children's Protection Society and in 1979 the Victorian State Government authorised CPS as a child protection agency under the Social Welfare Act 1970.Following the Carney Report of 1984, CPS formally relinquished its role and the Victorian Department of Community Services took over this role and function. My experiences with this wonderful secular society occurred in the temporary emergency care unit at Sale, Victoria.

The dates of my stays were 24/6/77-8/7/77, 22/1/79 2/7/79, 17/3/80-29/3/80, 29/5/80-18/6/80 and 14/12/81-22/12/81.

Another happy time I remember well occurred when I was in grade three, and we were living in Newborough in Victoria at that time.

I was quite good at gymnastic activities and enjoyed taking part in private gymnastic sessions which were probably organised through the community centre (as mum could not, and would not have paid for them!) Anyway, my specialty was on the uneven bars and my coach thought that I was really very good. I practised hard and eventually improved enough to be declared of competition standard. I was so *very* excited. Now I find that the outcome was totally predictable, but at the time I could not wait for him to discuss this prospect with mum and for them to enrol me in competitions. As soon as my coach approached my mother with this news, she put an instant stop to my gymnastics. I was devastated – but still remember the fun I had in this sport before it was spoiled for me. In high school I tried again to take up gymnastics, but I had lost my flexibility by then and did not continue the sport.

In grade four we resided in the town of Moe in Victoria. I became involved in the school play, called "The Rat Race." I loved it! After practising for absolutely ages at school, we children performed the show for a whole week, doing both afternoon matinees and evening shows. I have kept the program of the play and a video that was made, if only to remind me that I did in fact, enjoy a modicum of happiness as a child.

History & information about Australian orphanages, children's Homes & other institutions

VICTORIA - ORGANISATION

Swan House (1968 - 1979?)

From	1968
To	1979?
Categories	Children's Home, Home and Non-denominational

Swan House was a children's home in the town of Traralgon, established by the Victorian Society for the Prevention of Cruelty to Children in 1968. It provided temporary care for up to eight preschool and school age children. In 1971, Swan House relocated to a purpose-built facility in the town of Sale.

Admissions to Swan House were initially made for 3 months, with extensions to be made if the family situation had not improved. Swan House also operated as a temporary 'holding centre' for wards awaiting long term care arrangements. Children from the Latrobe Valley area thus did not have to be transferred to Allambie Reception Centre in Melbourne.

Swan House was located in rented property in Traralgon from 1968 to 1971. In 1971, a gift of land to the Children's Protection Society made it possible for Swan House to be moved to a purpose-built facility in the town of Sale. The Sale Swan House could accommodate up to 16 children.

Location

1968 Location - Swan House was located in Traralgon. Location: Traralgon

1971 Location - Swan House was located in Sale. Location: Sale

HAPPINESS

How can I describe happiness, when I don't know what it is?

But I know it lives at Swan House, with the staff and other kids.

I feel so safe! No danger here, no terrors in the night - grown-ups to give me cuddles and make the wrong things right.

I want to stay forever!

Why can't I just live here?

In a happy caring place in the absence of all fear.

I don't want my family to ever take me away.

Maybe THAT'S what happiness is! – Just peace, in every day.

Before innocence lost.

At 13 months of age.

Who would want to hurt this little girl?

The fear begins...

The house of my abuse in Morwell, Victoria

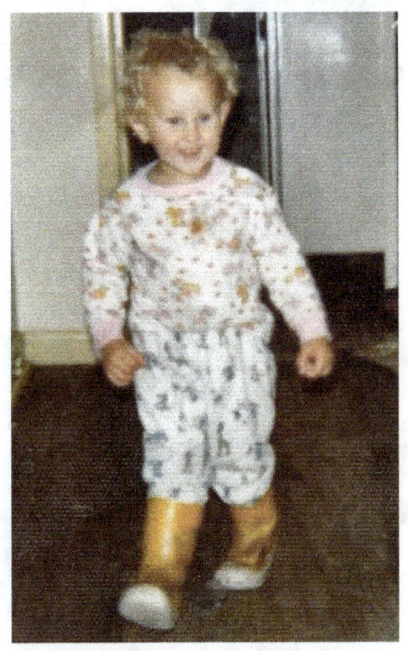

Oh, the innocence of a child…

I always felt alone

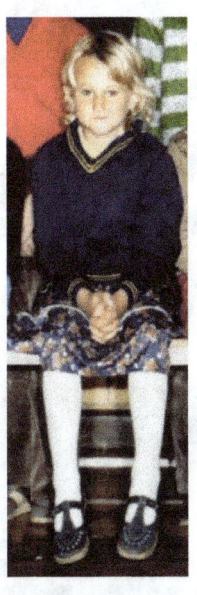

A picture of sadness and isolation

My happy South Australian holiday

The original Noel Parlane record cover

My Precious Bible

The back bedroom of this house in Moe, Victoria, was where much of my later sexual abuse occurred, prior to our move to Tasmania.

A very confused teenager

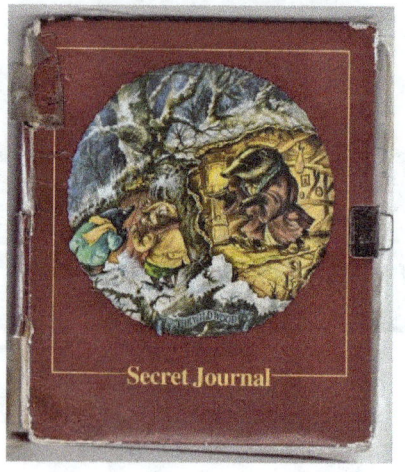

My diary

Chapter Three

And on it goes…

What a brave little girl I was, though I did not know it then. Throughout the remainder of my early years my sexual abuse continued relentlessly. It was not just the one or two horrific but isolated incidents but a hated part of my everyday life. I never knew when or how it would happen, just that it would happen as surely as night follows day. Looking back at 'that' little girl, I wonder how she survived the misery of having no-one to trust and nobody to whom she could turn for comfort. I really do. I think the only control I had in those years was to ensure that I was a 'good' girl – and I was a good girl. I tried so very hard at school work and at friendships so somebody – anybody, would like me. Now I wonder if that was such a good thing – had I been wilful and delinquent and obnoxious then perhaps people may have stopped to wonder why. As it was I was invisible and an easy target for my abusers. So long as I was a quiet and non-communicative child I slipped through the attention of teachers, doctors or anyone who may have provided me with solace and support. In short, anyone who might have picked up on the abuse I suffered and put a stop to it. But my journey through childhood was a lonely one and I had only myself to rely on. It is hard today, to envisage that nobody wondered why the skinny blonde child they were in contact with was always so sad – so very sad. My lack of trust and inability to get close to anyone, my constant injuries, my poor nutrition, and my tears were just not important to anyone, though I sincerely hope that my teachers and doctors did not harbour secret concerns which they did not follow up. I have no way of knowing now but if that was the case, it was a criminal failure on their behalf. It would have only taken one adult to stand up for me and voice their concerns to the relevant authorities for it all to stop and my life would have been very different.

Children, the elderly, and obviously animals are often totally powerless in the face of cruelty and evil and I have had many a good excuse to come to believe in the old saying by

Winston Churchill – (in the above context,)

"All that is needed for the triumph of evil is for good men to do nothing." *Children are not belongings!*

I am reminded of another Christmas time when I was aged thirteen or fourteen years. It is not one that I am ever likely to forget, nor I suppose will my little sister because she was there at the time. As I have already shared with you, I really have little understanding of my mother or the motivations for her behaviour. This of course, was one of those times.

Christmas as a family was never happy and it seemed that for mum, just spending it with her children was not ever something she wanted to do. I vividly remember her being most upset that she had not been invited out anywhere and so she was in a rage. She threw us all into the car and began speeding crazily down the road. It was a frightening experience for us but the worst thing of all was mum yelling out that she was going to kill us all because she did not care about herself or us. Due to the fear state that I was in, I don't remember why this did not actually happen – but it contributed to the general anxiety of my life and reinforced to me how little we mattered to our mother. I will never know whether she lost her nerve that day or was somehow prevented from fulfilling her threat, but I will never forget that Christmas Day for as long as I live. So I struggled on through these years, telling Bluey and my toy rabbit Snowballs my stories of woe as I hugged him to myself. It was a painful and confusing period of my life – as other children were developing a sense of identity, a set of values and a belief in a trust system, those things were alien to me. I had no 'centre,' no sense of who I was as a person and my only role models were my abusers and my neglectful, selfish and cruel mother. I went on to be confused about what values even were and was consumed with a self-loathing which I did not understand.

Chapter Four

A Happy Holiday

When I was in grade four at school, my mother met a man who seemed to be nice – at least he was not a predator or an abuser, so to me that qualified as nice... He took us on a holiday to Kingoonya, which is in outback South Australia near the goldfields. We stayed for two weeks and it was a happy time for us, fossicking and panning for gold and exploring the mines there. There was no power at the house so we relied on a generator and the toilet was an old mine shaft cavity. We children very much enjoyed the heat, the freedom and the great outdoors as well as the innocent expectation and fervent hope of finding gold. It was a happy and memorable holiday, for which I am very grateful. It's funny the things that implant on the memory... On the long, hot drive from Victoria to South Australia we listened to Charlie Pride on a cassette tape. Many years after this unusual holiday, and long after this man and mum broke up, I went to see Charlie Pride in concert and relived those memories. This concert was in Hobart

Tasmania, and I was lucky enough to get the great man to sign my ticket stub.

I still treasure that ticket stub.

Chapter Five

Seeking Solace

My nan was involved in the church so that from an early age whenever nan visited, she would take us along to the nearest one. When I was in grade three my family was living in Newborough, Victoria and through nana I was included in the activities of the Baptist church there. They were a wonderful group of people, missionaries from America and caring families who "took us in" and shared luncheons and opened their homes and hearts to us. Sometimes I was lucky enough to be taken to someone's house after church and not have to return home until the evening... My siblings were not so interested, but I had a great and desperate need to get away from home as much as possible and this was one way that as a child, I could manage that. This association continued until we moved to Tasmania, when I was in grade six. I guess that as a young girl I had little spiritual motivation to be involved, but certainly relished the opportunity to be around kind people and out of the house!

Soon after our move to Tasmania – in desperation at my plight and after some dreadful encounters with my mother – I decided that I had to earn money if I were ever to get out of my situation. As they clearly recall, I visited some people we knew there, arriving on their doorstep in a dishevelled state asking if I could do cleaning jobs in exchange for a little money. They agreed, so I did this on a regular basis. They remember sensing a fierce determination in me to better my life in some way and they also had a sense that I wanted to escape from something, but until recently they had no idea what or why.

Of course at that time I should have disclosed my abuse to them, as they were both kind and good-hearted people but my background had entrenched in me that nobody would understand or care about me and I did not want to upset them, so I pretended that nothing was wrong. Does this make me complicit in my own nightmare? An ignorant person might believe so, but that is the nature of the exploitation of children – they are conditioned to believe that the abuse is their own fault and have no power to believe that anything they say or do will affect any change in their own circumstances. And my conditioning had been intense and ongoing for many years by that time.

In the Christmas of that same year, all my efforts at making and saving money were shattered.

My mother had decided to purchase presents for the family and gave them to my brothers and sisters. There was no gift for me. The saddest part of this quite common oversight of me was that after my working and saving almost sixty dollars during that year, mum found out my bank details and took the lot. I only hope my siblings appreciated the gifts purchased with the sweat of my brow, but for me it was a devastating Christmas.

The couple I cleaned for introduced me to their church, and here I was befriended by another couple whom I would visit on many of the evenings that I just could not bear to be at home. They would often drive me home after dark but sometimes I was lucky enough to be allowed to stay with them overnight. How I used to wish that they had been my parents and that I could stay with them forever!

They were kind. As my birthday of that year approached, my elderly friends asked me what in the whole world would I like to receive – I had no hesitation in replying that my best present in the world would be a roast chicken – and so it was. How wonderful!

In my hideous life there were a handful of caring souls…

A CHILD'S LAMENT

What have I ever done to you, that you hurt me in this way?
For I am but a child, with no choices and no say.

I watch the other kids at play and just don't know what to do.
You've stolen all my innocence. I hope it pleases you.

Maybe you don't care what you've done, but my life is shattered.
A child destroyed at a tender age as if she never mattered.

Look down deep behind my eyes and see my unshed tears and know that you have caused my pain, my sorrow and my fears.

For these sad things won't leave me, as I struggle on alone
with no joy inside me – no heart to call my home.

The same lovely folk who gave me roast chicken for my birthday also invited me to share a Christmas lunch with them. I remember it well. I was allowed to go on condition that I took my younger sister along, which they welcomed because they badly wanted me to have a decent, hot meal. Bless that lovely family who gave me happy memories.

Throughout my young life, aside from my emotional reliance on my only friends Bluey the bear and Snowball the stuffed rabbit, I used to play with a set of farm animals that I would cut out from paper and stick on my bedroom wall. This was an outlet for my imagination and source of great comfort and enjoyment for me as I could at these times escape the horrors of my life and become immersed in fantasy. I would spend peaceful hours re-arranging the animals into different herds and paddocks and I was very kind to them, even if they were made of paper. I cared for them a lot as they were my refuge.

The other thing I did for many, many years in the solitude of my bedroom was to play a particular song over and over again. It really became the sound track to my life and barely a day would pass but that I would sit in my lonely room and listen to it constantly, crying and singing along with the feeling that it was written specifically for me.

I still have the original record, but I have not actually listened to it for thirty years – it is just too difficult to be transported back into the heart and mind of that sad, pathetic little girl that was me at the time.

The record was sung by a man called Noel Parlane, and the song which touched my heart was titled "Nobody's Child." Although it really concerns an orphan longing to be loved by a real family (which didn't happen because he was blind – so damaged,) I felt very damaged too and yearned for real love and caring for myself, *just as much as he did.*

NOBODY'S CHILD

Written by Hank Williams Jr.

"As I was slowly passin' an orphan's home one day, I stopped there for a moment just to watch the children play.

Alone a boy was standin' and when I asked him why, he turned with eyes that couldn't see and he began to cry.

Chorus

I'm nobody's child – I'm nobody's child, just like a flower I'm growing wild.

No mommy's kisses and no daddy's smiles. Nobody wants me, I'm nobody's child.

People come for children and take them for their own, but they all seem to pass me and I'm left here all alone.

I know they'd like to take me but when they see I'm blind, they always take some other child and I'm left behind.

(Chorus)

I'm nobody's child – I'm nobody's child, just like a flower I'm growing wild.

No mommy's kisses and no daddy's smiles, nobody wants me, I'm nobody's child.

No mommy's arms to hold me or soothe me when I cry, sometimes it gets so lonely here I wish that I could die. I'll walk the streets of Heaven where all the blind can see, and just like all the other kids there'd be a home for me.

(Chorus)

I'm nobody's child – I'm nobody's child, just like a flower I'm growing wild.

No mommy's kisses and no daddy's smiles, nobody wants me, I'm nobody's child."

At this stage of my young life, I really loved to attend church services each Sunday. I was searching for love and acceptance and a God with whom I belonged, who would look after me and deliver me from my hell. I have some heart breaking memories of sitting in our driveway back in the Victorian town of Moe – devastated at the times my mother would not allow me to go, crying uncontrollably and totally bereft. I still have my bible from that time and the verses I underlined upset me, even today.

"But God will redeem my soul from the power of the grave: for he shall receive me." (Book of Psalms – 49: 15.) There were many more, but most confusingly still, to me – *"Children, obey your parents in the Lord: for this is right."* (Book of Ephesians – 6: 1.)

I tried so hard to Believe, and to an extent gained some kind of comfort in my endeavours. I include my seeking out of religious faith in this story because it happened that way in my life but sadly for me I could never reconcile a God who was kind, all-knowing and forgiving with one who would allow such horrible abuse to happen to me without doing anything to help or rescue me.

I could not resolve this conundrum so I felt I was obviously not important to God either.

Chapter Six

The Final Horror

It is natural for me to remember well the occasion of the final sexual assault on my body. It was to represent a total change and a cornerstone in my life, just as living with constant abuse had been a normal aspect of my life previously.

It was during the September school holidays when I was almost thirteen years old that this episode occurred during a trip to Victoria. I was very happy to be 'going away' to stay with some friends from my old church – this was different to being dragged around as a child to different addresses and different states by my mother. The first week of the holiday was a relatively happy one staying with these friends and enjoying some normal activities. I remember the lack of stress and tension I felt during that week, it was delightful.

The second week however, was spent at the address of my mother's ex-partner. This practised violator somehow orchestrated this visit through my mother and decided that I was once again 'fair game' as I had been so many times before.

I recall that on this occasion I tried to express my disgust and refuse to allow the abuse to occur. Words of course meant nothing to him and so I attempted to thwart him physically, to no avail.

I clearly remember that during this assault at a stage that he was performing oral sex upon me by force, I tightened the grip of my legs against him. My hope and intention was that he would find it impossible to breathe in this situation. This was apparently the case as he abused me cruelly until I was forced to relax the grip. (An oxy-moron I know…)

Strange perhaps that this was the most vivid memory I have of the situation, which of course consisted of much worse for me! This episode and his further abuse signalled several things however. I was older now and *desperate* to have some say in what happened to me.

I couldn't take the exploitation and cruelty one second longer without protest, even at the risk of great and further harm to myself. I had had enough.

As I mentioned early in chapter two I cannot know whether the last episode of sexual abuse and rape was due to my developing body (risk of pregnancy and disclosure) or simply that I was getting older (paedophilia.) But other things were changing in my life at that time, which probably signalled my escape from abuse more than anything else.

I did not see my step-father again.

The sexual abuse and exploitation at the hands of those two particular men who had traumatised me my whole life had *finally ended!*

Later exploitation occurred as a result of my earlier treatment however, as I did not know love or self-respect, so I became an easy mark in my adult life for anyone who showed me the least affection. This was due to my belief back then (through my conditioning,) that to show fondness to a man meant nothing other than pleasing him sexually. More on that later…

WHO REALLY CARES?

Who really cares for me? Does anyone?
If so, who?
I know people say they care, but do they really mean it?
No. That's the answer.
"No."
No-one really cares for me, not really anyway.
If they did, why do they treat me like they do?
I CAN'T WIN.
I live an unfair life; cos no-one really cares for me.
They just walk away, or pretend they're listening.
I have a lot of problems
but no-one is interested in what they are. So I just keep them to myself, and I feel miserable
all the time. Please.
Just tell me.
Who REALLY cares?

Chapter Seven

Escaping Home

I was so very tired of the struggles with my mother that had been going on all my life (and even prior to that, with my struggle to be born!) It seemed that nothing I ever did or said was okay. She did not love me – in fact I am sure she hated me. How excruciating for a young daughter to endeavour to elicit her mother's love and approval in any and all ways possible and to receive constant rejection!

By the time I was fifteen years old I realised that my life with her was one of only grief and hopelessness for me. Looking back, I believe that because I was starting to mature I subconsciously was starting to realise that she had never treated me like a mother should, that she had allowed and encouraged bad things to happen to me and that this would never change. At the time I had a few casual hours work at a pizza shop, but not enough to survive on.

In the way of these things, my leaving home was the result of a relatively small incident – but it was the catalyst for us both.

Totally immersed in studying for my grade ten exams, I had forgotten to bring home from school a book my little sister apparently needed. This I did on two occasions. My mother screamed abuse at me this particular night and ordered me to pack my bags and get out of the house forever, before taking my little sister with her to attend her local pub for a darts competition.

I packed a bag and left. Just like that.

Cast out into a strange and frightening world alone, all I could feel was an overwhelming sense of injustice but more importantly, *RELIEF!*

Perhaps now my life and my body would be my own and I would find a place and time to rest, recover and begin the journey from wondering at the conflicting messages which had made up the fabric of my life thus far, towards some kind of healing.

The future, I have since realised, brings its own problems – different ones perhaps – but often reflecting past experiences and patterns. This was to become the way of my future for quite a long time to come, as you will see.

Having left home I moved in with a cousin for a short period of time before she moved on and I took over her lease.

It was a horrendously tough period for me, but a piece of cake compared to what I had already endured during my life. Naturally enough I managed to fail my school exams that year as I was still trying to work my casual hours, but I was so lucky that my school paid for me to attend the grade ten leaver's dinner so I could be included for the occasion.

I could not have attended college in any event as I had rent to pay and so had to concentrate on seeking more work. As I struggled on in this situation I found that I needed to rely heavily on charitable organisations such as the City Mission for a basic supply of food.

In desperation I applied for a 'Youth Homeless Allowance' but my mother told the authorities that it was I who had wanted to leave home and was welcome to return! (Her abuse of the truth may have been through her own fear I guess, as my young sister was still at home.)

Regardless, I was in a pickle as I watched other teenagers from good homes who merely wanted to leave home and party, receive this allowance whilst I had no home to return to and no money.

It is interesting to note at this point that a system set up in supposedly genuine good faith to help those in need could get it *so wrong*. By their very nature systems are impersonal, but yet again I felt betrayed when seeking genuine and much needed help. (More on systems a little later…)

I did eventually receive the homeless payment, many months later, on the strength of a rare supporting statement made by my sister to Social Security depicting the terrible state of my earlier home life. This money certainly helped me pay the rent and even purchase a modicum of my own food. A happy coincidence during that time was that I met a lovely and most helpful worker at the CES (a job agency,) who went out of his way to help me procure a job. In thanks I invited he and his partner for dinner – after my first pay of course! It was nice. When you have never had any kindness, it's the smallest nice things that can make the most difference in your life.

Chapter Eight

Disclosure!

Around six months before I was kicked out of home it became impossible to continue hiding the fact of my terrible personal problems from my school. A caring teacher there elicited from me the reasons why my home life was untenable and what my life had been like previously. She explained that there was a service which could help me, the Sexual Assault Support Service (SASS) and she personally took me there for assistance. I have a strong memory of that first visit – of wondering what the *hell* the lady who spoke to me at SASS could ever know about what I had been through. How could she give me advice and speak to me with knowledge gained only from books? Perhaps it was all too much for me at that stage, because I did not return for a very long time. I did eventually return to SASS which marked the beginning of many years of intermittent counselling, during which I struggled to make sense of my life of abuse. My feelings had never mattered before so it was difficult to even recognize or make sense of them, much less expose them to anyone. I found that the requirement of trust was at times way beyond what I was equipped to cope with, so it was easier to pretend that everything was okay and to leave.

After all this was my survival technique as a child – to rely only on myself and pretend things were okay, to just keep the peace and try to please others.

I found that I now desperately needed and wanted someone to rescue me, but not at the price of their pity. My walls were so high and I was so closed up that I truly believed I had to 'just get over it,' an expression I had heard all my life from my mother. It was a conundrum for me that I could assure a counsellor that really I was fine and be believed! How could I trust that person's judgement? In no way am I discrediting the wonderful people at SASS – in the end they helped me enormously – but they could do no more than that which I allowed.

A thought which continually assails me is that for a chronic victim of sexual abuse, the best and most effective way for the counsellor to discover what the victim's feelings really are would be to encourage them to keep a daily diary for a period of time. Abuse does not leave you – it haunts you in everyday life, day in and day out. It is much easier I believe for a 'blocked' person to express their feelings in this more remote way and for the counsellor to access them in that manner. After all, sexual abuse is built on secrecy and shame and it is the victim who is conditioned to the secrecy and who feels the shame.

THE SEXUAL ASSAULT SUPPORT SERVICE INC.
P.O. BOX 217, NORTH HOBART. 7000.
TELEPHONE (002) 31 1811

Report: Criminal Injuries Compensation Claim

Natasha

1. Outline Of Contact

Natasha first contacted the service in 1/11/89. She was referred by her school guidance officer who accompanied her.

More regular contact did not commence until Feb 1992 after which Natasha has had weekly or fortnightly appointments.

2. Assessment Of The Effects Of Sexual Assault

2.1 Emotional:

The most apparent effect of the assaults upon Natasha has been that of fear. She is afraid to live alone, and of being alone with men. She feels isolated and different, therefore finds it hard to make friends. She lacks self confidence. She experiences flashbacks of the abuse which have caused difficulties in developing a healthy sexual relationship and nightmares interrupt her sleep.

2.2 Education:

Natasha's lack of self confidence affected her ability to perform well at school. Her schooling ended when she was forced, by her mother, to leave the family home. Natasha was fifteen.

2.3 Housing:

Natasha is currently living with her boyfriend in his mother's home. Natasha has had to live independently since being forced to leave home at fifteen. She has had difficulty in finding suitable accommodation as her income was limited and she is frightened to live alone.

Her current accommodation is unsatisfactory and the people she lives with are unsupportive but her lack of confidence prevents her from making changes.

2.4 Family And Friends:

Natasha has had no significant contact with her family for three years. She felt unable to speak of the abuse when it occurred between the ages of five to thirteen. When she did seek help, her family became quite hostile towards her and she was forced to leave home. She says she had felt different and isolated since the abuse and has difficulty forming friendships and developing healthy relationships.

3 Summary

In my opinion, Natasha ▮▮▮▮ has suffered a considerable level of emotional trauma as a result of the sexual abuse she experienced as a child. The ongoing effects the abuse has had on her life include an inability to trust people, particularly men, low self esteem and a lack of self confidence, fear of living alone and of being alone with men. These effects are congruent with the common pattern of behaviour demonstrated by victims of child sexual abuse.

Chapter Nine

Police Involvement

At the age of sixteen, I had my own boyfriend. I sometimes stayed with him at his mother's house, when I feared being on my own.

I have a lot to relate on the effects of childhood sexual abuse on adult relationships, (including sexual encounters) but this is not the subject of this chapter – except to say that I confided in my boyfriend about the horror of my past. I was ready to accept some sympathy, support and understanding from him which I needed from someone so very, very badly. *He did not believe me!*

I am not sure why this was not the final straw in my unhappy life, as self-harm and self-hate had become an integral part of my existence by then. Indeed, when I was fifteen years old I could no longer see a reason to continue living and I attempted to kill myself, seriously wanting to end it all.

It was not a cry for help because I certainly believed that I was beyond any help that was available and not worthy of it anyway. My cousin's boyfriend thwarted my efforts and he made me promise that I would not attempt suicide again.

Looking back, I naturally feel grateful for his interference but recognise a huge mistake made. *Anyone* who attempts to end their own life needs professional help immediately! I survived, but to be at that point – no matter whom it is – immediate hospitalisation and treatment is necessary and the only way forward. Every single time, make no mistake!

Back to the boyfriend! Not only did he not believe the story of my miserable life but he set me a challenge – that if I truly was telling him the truth, then I should go to the police and report my abuse to them.

It did not occur to me to refuse, as the abuse was real, it happened the way I had explained and I wanted to please him by doing as he asked… So I did.

Thus began what was to be one of the most painful experiences imaginable – I had never felt more alone in my entire life and found the system overwhelming (to say the least.) I struggled through so many interviews and statements at the police station which were harrowing, embarrassing and exhausting and would be dropped home afterwards to my flat to try to deal with my raw emotions and the memories which erupted like a volcano at these times – totally alone and without a support person of any kind.

The boyfriend who demanded I take the action was nowhere to be found during this gruelling process and when I did see him, I tired of his whimper that he 'didn't know what to do.' *Who did?* I was riding a rollercoaster of emotions and heartache and as always, there was only me.

One of the detectives I was working with was very good to me, sensitively advising that the investigation should proceed at a pace with which I could cope. I have not cried in front of anyone so much as her, before or since. I cry a lot by myself but I allowed the tears to flow many times with her. My association with the police to bring my abusers to task and to have them both charged took several arduous years. I still lacked even basic confidence and part of me felt that I was not worthy of their time and attention. Once entered into the system however, I did not have the option of cringing away on the premise that what had happened to me in my young life did not matter. Later in my story you will have the chance to see some of the police reports which were written during that time. Now, I wonder where I found the strength to deal with this myriad of strangers, most of who were men, and repeatedly relive in my mind every episode of sexual exploitation and abuse which had been perpetrated against me.

I was constantly embarrassed, ashamed and frightened. After all, I had not suddenly become an avenging survivor with a mission to bring bad people to justice – I was still a terrified, conditioned little girl without the skills to stand up for myself.

I did it all simply to please my boyfriend!

I guess this was a result of my upbringing – men's desires were paramount and I was powerless to refuse their needs. Had I been further along the path to healing I believe I would have coped with the legal system with more confidence, conviction and aplomb. I knew that what had been inflicted upon me in my young life was criminally wrong – but I never had any evidence to rely on that my life mattered to anyone.

The next shocking thing to relate is that after working through this new living nightmare, I was told that it was unlikely that charges would ever be made against my abusers. What a validation that the crimes against me did not warrant attention and that my traumatised life mattered *nothing at all* to anyone!

What *the HELL* did I expect?

Being realistic, it could be said that this was due to a lack of firm evidence to support my allegations and that the crimes had occurred in my past. My sister had admitted to being raped by the same two men to police (in addition to me,) yet balked at the idea of supporting me in a Court situation. Mum claims she was interviewed by police and stated that she had a feeling something was going on, but knew not what to do. Apparently my younger sister was not questioned at all, which I only recently found out!

All are entitled to their own response to sexual abuse and exploitation as it is a crime visited upon them, and people cope or block out this crime according to their own character and circumstances. Perhaps it would have all been too traumatic for them at the time, or at least too embarrassing. I will never know, but at the time I felt immensely let down by yet another system and other members of my own family with whom I could have shared support and vindication.

During my later years of abuse I kept a diary and the police had access to this account of my life wherein abuse was mentioned continuously, but alone, it was not enough to secure a conviction.

After all, little girls have wild imaginations and suffer flights of fancy – don't they?

My diary, from which the following entries are taken;

Dear diary,

(Name removed) knows what happened back in May. He said he is going to kill the other person involved. Even if it did happen before I knew him. This person shouldn't have touched me like he did or held me tightly against the wall.

Natasha. 16th Oct, 1989. (15yrs 11 m.)

Dear diary,

(Boy) is the best thing that has happened to me, but he wants me to give him head so much. I haven't done it for about ten years. The first time I hated it and I was forced to do that and everything else that happened. I hate those people but I love him. Natasha. 23rd Oct, 89. (15yrs 11 m.)

Dear diary,

Next Wednesday afternoon I've got an appt. at SASS, the social worker from school is taking me. I have to tell them everything that happened in Victoria, and everything that happened on the 13th of May. They're going to make me see that none of it was any of my fault and try to make me forget about it. (Several unrelated comments follow.) *I've been hurt far too many times by men in my life ever since I was a few years old and if I ever get hurt once more by anyone I will kill myself because I don't know how much more I can take. That is a promise* I WILL KEEP. *Natasha.* 26th Oct, 1989. (15yrs 11 m.)

Not much flight of fancy happening there, wouldn't you agree?

I now understand how the legal system works and that my thoughts to myself on paper just did not cut the mustard. Whilst looking back through my diary of that particular year I found some other entries which still have the power to make me weep – though largely unrelated to the police investigation.

Dear diary,

Tonight I am at home by myself and I am not in a very good mood and I feel like I don't have a friend in the world. I hope I'm going to die soon...I'm not going to die happy because why should I when my mother hates me. Some people at school are also turning against me. The only boy I have ever really loved so much also dislikes me, I'm sure my neighbours also hate me...I just wish I was someone different and had friends and people around me I can trust. Natasha. 27th July, 1988. (14yrs 8m.)

Dear diary,

Today, at school Mr (teacher) said that if we had a problem, whether it be money, parents etc. we could go and see him or Mrs (grade co-ordinator.) He had no right to say that because he doesn't know how poor people are.

I bet he'd never guess that we were poor.

At least I'm sure he always had food to eat, unlike me. Sometimes we have it to eat but I like fresh bread and cold milk for breakfast. I could go and see one of them but they wouldn't be able to spare a whole day listening to all my problems. I wish there was someone I could talk to because I just keep my problems to myself, and believe me, it isn't a very good thing to do because you always feel depressed and HATED and inferior. Natasha. 16th March, 1989. (15yrs 4m.)

Dear diary,

Well, – it's pretty boring at the moment... except for the fact that every time I am happy mum seems to make me miserable. She has been trying to get me and (name removed) together for some time. If, which means never, (name removed) asked me to go out with him – he's not that blind – and I got happy mum would probably make me miserable by saying I wasn't allowed to see him again. But that's life! I'm sure I will survive being miserable all my life.

Natasha. 15th July, 1989. (15yrs 8m.)

Dear diary,

I'm my old self again, miserable. (Current boy fancied) didn't mean it when he said he loved me last night. He only said it to get what he wanted. I'm testing myself now, I'm seeing if I can go one week without eating.

I don't care if I starve myself, no-one else would. I'm very seriously thinking about it, what's the point of living if you're going to be miserable all your life and no one to love you. Believe you me it is a fucking rotten life and no-one should be like I am. Natasha. 27th July, 1989. (15yrs 8m.)

Dear diary,

I wish I didn't like (name removed) so much because then I could probably see that he's no friend of mine. On Saturday night while I was at work I asked (name removed) if he had a gun, so he can shoot me, because I wanted to die. I don't need a gun now because I've got my tablets mum bought me... I've got thirty of them. I'm not that foolish though, that's the problem. Natasha.

29th August, 1989. (15yrs 9m.)

Dear diary,

To-night (name removed) told me that my mum is going to try and take my Austudy money from me next year. She said that she will lose enough money when I leave home as it is. She's got my Austudy form too, so somehow I have to get to town to get another form. All she is a fucking fat slut who talks out of her arse. Natasha. 8th September, 1989. (15yrs 10m.)

Dear diary,

Last night ...she mentioned to him that I haven't been eating lately, he said that is probably why I am getting sick all the time. If you ask me I think I'm getting sick because of the state the house is in. Maybe I would eat more if mum bought food for us to eat. Natasha. 12th September, 1989. (15yrs 10m.)

What a poor, sad, confused and neglected little girl I was then – wracked with emotional pain, grief and guilt. Perusing my old diary entries transports me, back to those moments like nothing else can and they are moments I would wish upon no-one else, ever. Most of the rest of the diary contains the confusion of a damaged teenager seeking the affection of boys, not unusual for a girl of fifteen. But I was a girl who had not known love or affection and who believed that I did not matter to anyone, least of all myself. This is illustrated as follows;

Dear diary,

There is one good thing about (name removed) and that is that he hated to hurt me. The time he hurt me was bad enough for him – that was when he got off with two others while I was watching. Natasha.

7th November 1989. (15yrs 11m.)

Bad enough for *HIM!* Thank God I have made some progress since then, but the non-development of a sense of self and self-respect through continuous years of being treated like a plaything against your will takes much getting over. Back to the subject of this particular chapter!

Although the decision was made by the authorities that they did not have the ability to procure enough evidence to charge my two main abusers, it turned out that there was another hurdle with which I could contend to bring them both to account. It was explained to me that I could sue my abusers and should they not have compensation with which to pay, then I could apply to receive what was called Criminal Injuries Compensation.

Of course money was not the bloody point! I grappled with that idea until I finally realised that by going ahead with litigation in this manner they would still be exposed as the criminals they were and also they would know that I was seeking redress for the wrongs they had caused.

It was probably fortunate that I had never had anything come easily to me so far in my life, because I had the grit and determination to rise up once again after being let down and just get on with it, as I have always done.

OFFICE OF DIRECTOR OF PUBLIC PROSECUTIONS

INQU~~~~
OUR REF 52849 J:B
YOUR REF:

20 September, 1994

Mr. ▓▓▓,
Legal Aid Commission of Tasmania,
123 Collins Street,
HOBART

Dear Sir,

RE: NATASHA ▓▓▓

The vast majority of the alleged crimes occurred in Victoria where the alleged offenders reside.

Both Victorian and Tasmanian Police have extensively and at considerable expense investigated these complaints. I agree with them that no charges should be laid.

If your client seeks civil redress I suggest that she should sue the men. Apart from anything else that will, to some degree, bring home to the offenders something of what they have (allegedly) done. Their names and addresses are - ▓▓▓
▓▓▓, Morwell, and ▓▓▓, Yallourn North. Both Victoria.

Should a judgment be obtained against either in respect of Victorian crimes but not satisfied then I would suggest that you look to the Victorian compensation scheme.

Only 3 incidents are alleged in Tasmania - and all against Mr. ▓▓▓. If a civil judgment is obtained against him in respect of those but not satisfied then we would not oppose an award under the Tasmanian Act.

A large number of crimes are alleged. If all allegations are correct then substantial damages are due. But the alleged Tasmanian crimes fit as only a small proportion and we would be opposed to them being treated otherwise.

Your client's sister ▓▓▓ did say that she had been raped by both men. Also that she would not give evidence.

Two women, as they now are, named ▓▓▓ have been tracked down by Police. Your client suggested that they may have been victims. Both deny any crimes were committed on them.

A doctor in Victoria has advised that he examined your client 16 times between 1977 and 1983 but that no sexual abuse was ever mentioned.

Your client has stated that she reported sexual assault to her supervisor at ▬▬▬▬. That lady recalls no such report.

Yours faithfully,

▬▬▬▬▬▬▬

PRINCIPAL CROWN COUNSEL

Chapter Ten

The Hearings

In December of the year 1994 when I was a mere twenty-one years old, I travelled to Melbourne, Victoria to attend the first Tribunal Hearing. I remember standing outside the Flinders St Station feeling totally overwhelmed as I had no idea what was going to happen or what to expect. This hearing was being held in Victoria as this was the state in which much of my sexual abuse had occurred. All I knew through my lawyers in Tasmania was that now the abusers in fact did *NOT* have to be notified of the action I was undertaking and that investigations had revealed that they had little income or the means to be sued for property. What a state I was in! I had desperately wanted my boyfriend to make this journey with me (yes, the same one who had challenged me to go to the police years before) but he did not come. Alone again, naturally...

I had no option but to stay with my mother who was again living in Victoria at that time – not a happy situation for me at all. I remember the horror of the peak hour traffic and the difficulty of procuring a taxi at that hour of the morning in the city, but mostly the overpowering anxiety of attending the court.

Once I arrived at the courthouse I was really not much better off because I found the proceedings incredibly difficult to follow and to understand. In fear and trepidation, I watched the proceedings unfold before me, but in conclusion it transpired that I was awarded the maximum amount possible for the crimes against me under the Criminal Injuries Compensation Law which was in place during the years of my abuse. This amounted to a grand total of twenty thousand dollars, ten thousand dollars for each of my perpetrators.

Twenty thousand dollars may sound like quite a lot of money to be given in such a way, but just stop and think. Eight horrific years of my life were worth a mere twenty grand – which equates to two thousand five hundred dollars *per year* for my suffering. Whilst of course I was grateful and felt somewhat vindicated, I realised once more how systems are so out of touch with the reality of a victim's life. At the time of this award I was also required to sign a document which I didn't understand at the time, but my signature apparently has prevented me from pursuing any further form of prosecution against these two barbaric men at any stage in the future. My only hope therefore was that one day in their lives these bastards would get what they truly deserved!

I used my compensation money for a deposit on a home in Tasmania. I so badly wanted a home to call my own, filled with sunlight and peace and protected from all fear and harm to those who dwelt within. It was an exciting prospect and one which gave me great joy at the time.

I have already explained that the effects of abuse continue long after the abuse itself has stopped. As a teenager, I still sought love and affection to the detriment of my own best interests (which by the time of writing I am trying very hard to avoid doing.) So that, against sensible legal advice given to me at the time I made the decision to buy a house in joint names along with my unsupportive boyfriend of four years. I was just so very naïve as to the ways of the world and foremost in my mind was my need for someone to love and to love me back. How wrong I was, as things turned out...

After settling into my first ever home, I felt confident enough to seek recompense from one of my perpetrators under Tasmanian law as I had been sexually abused and exploited in that state in the mid – eighties. Due to the Tasmanian system of law this perpetrator needed to in fact be notified of my action.

Through investigations undertaken I was horrified to learn that he had married and had two young step-children in his care. I was devastated! What kind of suffering were those poor little souls going through, I agonised – as I knew he would begin violating the little girl if he had not begun to already... I later learned that his wife and children had left the family home, never to return.

I would like to think that my exposure of him as an abuser caused this to happen, I don't know – but at least my actions may have saved another little girl from a life of horror. Approximately nine months later, when I was still twenty-one years old I attended a hearing in the courts in Tasmania. As a result of these proceedings I was awarded a sum of money in compensation for the abuse I had suffered in that state. More vindication I guess, and at least in this instance there occurred exposure of the abuser – which, as I have already mentioned, may have saved another little girl from a life like mine. However, there is a dark side to all of these court actions. As the police could not garner enough hard evidence to convict and imprison my perpetrators in either Tasmania or Victoria, these two men are still free to traumatise other young lives, which they are undoubtedly doing with abandon.

I have pursued the legal and court systems as far as possible through every avenue open to me, and it still wasn't enough.

I cannot stop them.

I believe things may have turned out quite differently had my sisters come forward in corroboration but all I can conceivably do is wait and hope that someone else comes forward to have them both prosecuted – another victim with perhaps a support network behind her or a caring mother, teacher, preacher or friend who is prepared to notice her dilemma and step up for her.

I have done all I can.

IAN SALE FRANZCP

prov. no. 26707BK

ACN 009 530 518

SECOND FLOOR,
7 FRANKLIN WHARF
HOBART

GPO BOX 1577 HOBART 7001

TEL 31-0530 FAX 34-8473

Legal Aid Commission of Tasmania
GPO Box 9898
HOBART 7001

14th January 1993

Your ref. RB/RR - 92H130625

Dear Sirs,

Re: Natasha ▓▓▓▓▓

Thank you for asking me to provide this assessment. I interviewed Ms ▓▓▓ on the 13th January 1993 as arranged. I understand that Ms ▓▓▓ is making an application for Criminal Injuries Compensation in Tasmania and Victoria, arising out of her being subject to prolonged and repetitive childhood sexual abuse.

Natasha ▓▓▓ is a 19 year old resident of ▓▓▓▓, living with her boyfriend and his mother. She currently works as a receptionist in a government agency.

Her family background is complex. This arises out of her mother's multiple relationships. Her mother has had four children in total, by three men. In addition she has a lengthy association with ▓▓▓▓▓, one of the perpetrators of sexual victimisation upon your client.

Ms ▓▓▓ became subject to sexual abuse from the age of 5 years. This abuse occurred in two quarters. The major perpetrator was her mother's de facto husband ▓▓▓▓. He sexually assaulted her on a regular basis from when she was aged 5 up to when she was aged 13 years. This abuse initially consisted of fondling or touching behaviours but quickly escalated to include oral and vaginal sex, probably from the age of 7 years.

The other perpetrator was a man named ▓▓▓▓▓, described as a friend of the household. The incidents involving ▓▓▓ were fewer, and probably confined to a period when she was aged 5 years to 7 years. However, as with ▓▓▓, the behaviours included sexual intercourse.

Ms ▓▓▓ had a poor relationship with her mother. Her mother clearly has an unusual personality, self-centred and immature. Her mother had, from an early stage told your client that she was unwanted, that she was a mistake, etc., etc. As you are probably aware, children more often than not fail to disclose sexual abuse. In this particular situation, given the problematical relationship with her mother, her failure to disclose is entirely unsurprising. There were no other people she might have been able to speak to. Furthermore, the abuse occurred at an early age such that she may not have believed there was anything wrong or unusual with what was happening, and further, believed that it happened to everybody.

Ms ▮▮▮ would have manifest many of the features of the so-called Childhood Sexual Abuse Accommodation Syndrome. This is a term describing a pattern of behaviour characteristic of children who are being repetitively sexually abused by someone they would ordinarily trust, e.g. a member of the same household. The syndrome is characterised by secrecy and guilt on the child's part, so that they see themselves more as an accomplice rather than a victim, and thus there is usually a failure to disclose. They feel extraordinary powerless, unable to directly resist the advances of the perpetrator. The child will often maintain a façade of normalcy, thus the "accommodation", but this is often at considerable emotion cost.

Sexual abuse stopped when Ms. ▮▮▮ was aged approximately thirteen years. At this time the household moved to Tasmania. Her relationship with her mother remained poor, and she eventually left home when aged fifteen. It was around this time that she first approached the Sexual Assault Support Service for assistance. More recently she has reported her situation to Police. I understand that Police enquiries are continuing.

She is now in a steady relationship and has achieved steady employment.

During the interview she was noted to be shy and anxious to the point of timidity. She had obvious difficulties recounting some features in the history, and was not pressed. As the interview progressed she became more confident and expressed a wish to be able to do something for those subject to sexual abuse.

Comment

This young woman was subject to repetitive sexual abuse including sexual intercourse from an early age. There were two perpetrators, one of whom was a member of her household. The abuse spanned a period of approximately eight years.

The sexual abuse of this young woman occurred in the context of a markedly dysfunctional family. Her mother seemed to have significant personality difficulties, and Ms. ▮▮▮'s upbringing was characterised by a lack of security and frequent rejection. In such circumstances it is difficult to tease apart the effects of the sexual abuse from the effects of her dysfunctional mother. However, the problems overlap as her mother's problems were likely a factor in the aetiology of the sexual abuse. As a child she appears to have been left in situations of potential hazard repeatedly, and there is some possibility that her mother was aware that inappropriate behaviours were occurring.

As an adult, Ms ▮▮▮ is a particularly shy and anxious young woman, very apprehensive at being alone, and markedly unassertive. She has a low self-esteem. She thus has a rather avoidant personality, and this likely flows from both the pathological effect of her mother and the repetitive sexual abuse.

One specific consequence of the sexual abuse has been the effects upon her current relationship. She is anxious and possessive in this relationship, readily fearing that her partner will be unfaithful. She holds an assumption that males in general are likely to be sexually predatory. She has also experienced difficulties in her sexual relationship. These difficulties have been concealed from her boyfriend. Initially she had extreme difficulty in coping with any form of physical contact, but has generally overcome this. Nonetheless there are still times when she becomes very anxious and agitated in relation to physical contact. She gains little if any satisfaction out of sexual behaviour, and some sexual behaviours cause her considerable distress. She is readily reminded of the previous contacts with her victimizers, and the abnormal sexual behaviour involved.

She has a chronically impaired sleep pattern with a tendency to frequent nightmares, often relating in content to the previous abuse. She continues to fear the two perpetrators, and has a general fear that she may be subject to another sexual assault.

She is receiving counselling from the Sexual Assault Support Service and this has obviously assisted her to a degree. I would recommend that this continue. I understand that there may be some group therapy involvement through that service, and I think this would be potentially very helpful for her.

In addition, there may be some value in her seeing a clinical psychologist or psychiatrist at some stage. Her unassertiveness and shyness are particular problems for her, and there may be scope for cognitive behavioural therapy to address these difficulties, allowing her to attain a greater degree of personal autonomy.

Please do not hesitate to contact me should you require clarification or additional information.

Yours faithfully,

Ian Sale FRANZCP

IAN SALE FRANZCP

SECOND FLOOR,
7 FRANKLIN WHARF
HOBART

prov. no. 26707BK
ACN 009 530 518

GPO BOX 1577 HOBART 7001
TEL 31-0530 FAX 34-8473

Legal Aid Commission of Tasmania
GPO Box 9898
HOBART 7001

22nd March 1993

Dear Sirs,

Re: Natasha

Further to your recent telephone call, I have reviewed my file on your above-named client. I had not realised initially that there would be jurisdiction problems in relation to her claim for Criminal Injuries Compensation, and I had initially seen her case as one of representing pervasive sexual abuse spanning several years, and the precise location was of no great importance in regard to the clinical effects.

Examination of her statement reveals that the great majority of the offences against her occurred in Victoria. It was in Victoria where the abuse by the two men concerned commenced, and continued until she left Victoria in 1984. Subsequent to that date there were then approximately 3 incidents of sexual assault occurring in Tasmania in 1986. These Tasmanian incidents were perpetrated by one of the original assailants.

While trying to tease apart the effects of the different locations is somewhat artificial, it is readily apparent that the abuse was initiated in Victoria, and there were much greater number of specific incidents in that state. I would therefore see her "Victorian experiences" as having played the major part in her current difficulties.

In other words, had the Tasmanian incidents not occurred, I believe her clinical situation would be much the same as it currently is. If any specific effect flowed from the Tasmanian offences, it would have been confined to an increase in her sense of helplessness and lack of safety, wherever she might be.

I trust this answers your enquiries. I enclose my curriculum vitae as requested.

Yours faithfully,

IAN SALE FRANZCP

SO ALONE

Why am I always so alone, so scared, so sad, so lost?

The bad things you have done to me have come at such a cost.

I see my friends all laughing so happy and carefree, and I know I cannot join them, this cannot be me.

My laughter has been stolen my smile long cast away.

My childhood spent in misery and I'll fight to make you pay!

I'm used to fear don't worry so I'll face the courts alone.

To survive I need the knowledge for your crimes that you atone.

It's not about the dollars,

I'd rather see you rot in Hell but to save the other kids out there,

Jail will do just as well!

HOWIE & MAHER

BARRISTERS & SOLICITORS

ACCREDITED FAMILY LAW SPECIALIST

ASSOCIATE:

3RD FLOOR
116 HARDWARE STREET
MELBOURNE, VICTORIA 3000

POSTAL ADDRESS
BOX 4756, G.P.O.
MELBOURNE, VIC. 3001
AUSDOC DX 265

TELEPHONE (03) 642 0499

FACSIMILE (03) 642 2070

OUR REF: FAB:930373

YOUR REF:

17 January, 1995

Ms. Natasha ,
,
MOONAH EAST. TAS 7007

Dear Natasha,

Re: Application to Crimes Compensation Tribunal

We confirm the appearance of upon your behalf at the Crimes Compensation Tribunal on 12 December, 1994 before Magistrate Harding. We confirm that an award was made in your favour for a total of $20,000.00 in accordance with the enclosed Statement. You should receive this award by cheque within the next six weeks.

Further an award for your costs was made in the total sum of $3,097.50 in accordance with the enclosed statement. We therefore enclose our account which has been paid by the Tribunal.

As this matter is now completed we will close our file. Please note, however, that if your physical or emotional wellbeing deteriorates, or if you suffer further expenses or pecuniary loss, you may be entitled to seek further compensation from the Tribunal. There is a six year time limit upon these types of claims. Please do not hesitate to contact our office should you have any queries.

Please do not hesitate to contact our office should you have any queries or require any further assistance with respect to any of your other legal requirements. We enclose our brochure detailing some of the other services we offer. In particular, and without wishing to appear presumptuous, we bring to your attention the desirability of having an up-to-date Will. We would also be happy to render assistance to you if you so require with respect to the prudent investment of your award.

....cont/2

We take this opportunity now to thank you for your instructions.

Yours faithfully
HOWIE & MAHER

20 January 1995

Miss N███████
███████
EAST MOONAH 7009

Dear Natasha

Re: Criminal Injuries Compensation - Tasmanian claim

We refer to your attendance at our offices on the 17th January 1995 and acknowledge receipt of your file from the Legal Aid Commission. Thank you again for instructing us to act on your behalf

We have now had an opportunity to read your file and become familiar with its contents. We agree with Mr ███████ that now your Victorian application has been successful, we should pursue further compensation through the Tasmanian scheme.

The Tasmanian Legislation governing criminal injuries compensation is a little different to that which applies in Victoria. The Tasmanian Legislation provides that before the Master can determine whether compensation is payable or not, he must be satisfied that a victim cannot pursue any other remedy against the offender. There is no such provision in the Victorian Legislation.

Therefore, if the offender has any property of value and it is possible to sue them for a civil action such as assault, then that avenue must be taken first before an application can be made for criminal injuries compensation. If an offender has no assets, usually this threshold question can be overcome easily because it can be argued that even if a victim does sue, then nothing is likely to result. We expect that this will be the senario in your case.

It will therefore be necessary to obtain some financial information on ███████. We shall have to write to him advising him that we are to issue proceedings against him and request that he provide us with some information as to his financial affairs. We shall of course explain to him that if he has no assets then we shall not proceed. We anticipate that give this, he shall respond to our request. We shall also undertake several searches in Victoria to ascertain whether he has any real property (i.e. land) or whether he is bankrupt. Before we do this however, we wish to speak with you again to ascertain whether you have any further information that could assist us in this regard.

In familiarising ourselves with the file, we also took the opportunity of discussing the matter with ███████ was appalled at the nonattention your matter attracted from the Victorian Police and considers that she would have a basis upon which to request that your file be reviewed by the Director of Public Prosecutions in Victoria with the view to them recommending upon the review of the file that further investigations be undertaken. ▮ advised the writer that the Police have not seen fit to even interview the offenders. This is somewhat unusual and may attract the DPP's attention and interest in reopening the file. Of course, if you requested the matter be pursued, this may lead to further involvement in the criminal procedures in Victoria.

Would you please make a further appointment with the writer at your convenience to discuss these matters. We look forward to seeing you again soon.

Yours faithfully,

per:

There are several interesting things of note within the previous reports, which I think deserve to be brought to attention, as I am not the only person who has had to tread this path and there will be others behind me who will have to as well. These things signify the vast chasm between what happens in real life and the manner in which the law deals with abuse such as mine.

Firstly, in Dr Sale's covering letter to his report he makes a very interesting and valid point. "The precise location (of the abuse) was of no great importance in regard to the clinical effects." How true! And yet in legal parlance these sorts of details take precedence over all other considerations. This situation has the power to make a victim feel even more demeaned and confused than he or she already does. In the letter from my Tasmanian firm of lawyers it is noted that a lawyer *"was appalled at the non-attention your matter attracted from the Victorian police...the police have not seen fit to even interview the offenders...this is somewhat unusual..."*

All I can surmise from this distressing fact is that my case was not handled well or properly by the police. I have to wonder why.

If it was because I was still young and powerless with no support system (or money, or 'name' behind me) then an injustice has certainly been done.

How can this be allowed to happen? No wonder many abuse victims feel that it is just too hard to come forward to try to bring their perpetrators to justice.

There was none for me.

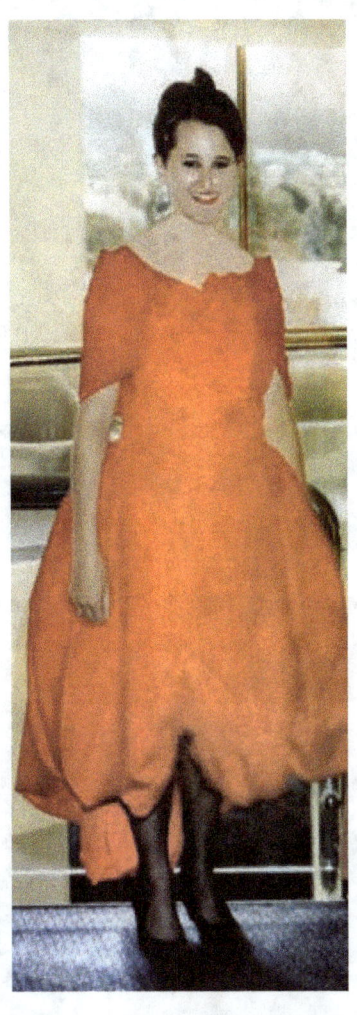

*Me, as an entrant in the Miss Tasmania Quest.
Amazing what a pretty dress and a big smile can hide...*

I thought this ceremony would make me safe

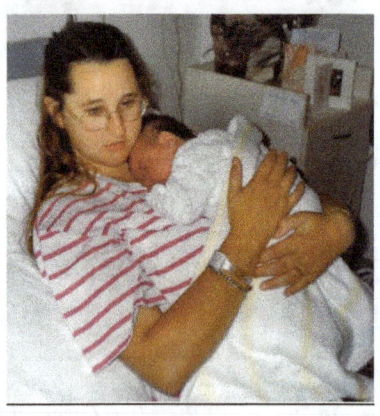

The birth of my daughter

My beloved daughter Madelyn and me!

During the time of my gambling addiction

Chapter Eleven

Benjy and Brothers

In order to illustrate my general confusion about men in general, I have another little anecdote to relate. At some point during my tortured childhood, my family moved into an area where we inherited a neighbour, an elderly man who lived alone and shared his life with a cute little dog called Benjy. I loved that little dog and the fact that I was invited over for cruskits and cheese and at times even ice-cream! These were happy interludes for me at the time and it was a new experience for me to be in the company of somebody kind who seemed to want nothing from me and who allowed me to spend happy times with the little dog. After we moved away I heard from my mum that my old friend had died. She told me that apparently he wanted me to have his little dog. Imagine! My own little dog! Probably as you would predict, I was not able to honour my friend's wishes. But the horrible crux of the story is this – before we moved away, standing at the boot of the family car, my stepfather demanded to know if the old man had touched me in the way that HE did! What the *hell* was my stepfather going on about?

Wanting to provide solace to me for the apparent abuse of another when he himself carried out such abuse on me regularly and viciously? I did not understand, but was most upset. I don't know what became of poor Benjy as my family had moved on again, and as a child I had no way of determining what happened to my elderly friend either. I was devastated. On so very many levels, my mind was in turmoil – the elderly neighbour was a nice old man and my friend – he had not done anything to me, except to be kind.

No *wonder* I was confused and trusted no-one! An extremely ugly and frightening footnote for me to the story of Benjy is that I was informed only last year that my elderly former friend and neighbour had apparently been murdered – supposedly because he really was a "paedophile" … I do not believe that he was.

Could I rely on nothing in this world? Was nothing true, or as it seemed? I felt then, and still do today, a strange and ominous sense of unease whenever I recall this episode in my life. I have also yet to mention my brother and step-brother and the place they had in the development of my confused and warped idea of men and their motivations. My real brother I cared about, but my mother told me that she could not cope with him and his behaviour and when he was around thirteen years old he was sent away to live with relatives in Tasmania.

I often wonder if his behaviour was an 'acting out' of sorts because of the horrors he must have been aware of, occurring under his nose at home.

What an understandable reaction if that was the case, as he was a mere child with no more power than I had to affect or modify the behaviour of the adults around him. I was the victim, but felt guilty on his behalf at the turn his life had taken. This feeling of hyper-responsibility for the happiness or otherwise of others I suspect came from the belief that my own feelings did not matter – a direct result of my abuse. My step-brother was a different 'kettle of fish' in that he appeared to take metaphorical lessons from his own father. I should perhaps feel pity for him, but I don't and *never* will. I remember clearly this young man trying to persuade me to let him touch me sexually, with the reasoning; *"Well, dad does!"* I allowed no abuse from this quarter, as I was a little older by that stage. From him I learned that I should trust no-one of the male gender and that I was merely as valuable as a cheap bottle of wine which gets passed around from one man to another.

What a mixed up, desperate for love and desperate to avoid it teenager I had become!

Chapter Twelve

The Miss Tasmania Quest

An illustration of the turmoil of these times for me was that I continued to believe that a good life is one which is devoted to those 'less fortunate'. God only knows where that sentiment came from, as I had precious little example of this in my own circumstances! As I grappled with the realisation that I had been a victim of terrible abuse all my life, I did not want to wallow in self-pity. Helping others seemed like the right thing to do, now that I could make my own choices, so I entered the Miss Tasmania Quest. I had no sponsors, but raised a large amount of money for what was then known as the 'Spastic's Association'. I found it incredibly uplifting to meet the other girls who worked so hard for good causes and to feel a part of the greater good going on. It was also a personal test for my confidence as I was painfully shy, self-conscious and hated attention of any sort. Needless to say I did not become Miss Tasmania, but the money I raised helped a good cause and it was a positive experience which I had generated for myself. I still do grapple with shyness and putting myself forward, but as always I do not try to hide from that which is difficult or demanding.

Chapter Thirteen

The Bride

Apart from normal teenage schoolgirl crushes already reported earlier from my diary (not that I had the ability to respond to them normally!) my first steady love was my boyfriend who stayed around from the time I was sixteen. I had no healthy relationship markers or experience and still carried that hyper-sensitive need to carry the responsibility for others' happiness.

At the tender age of sixteen my desperate need for affection resulted in my first pregnancy with him, which neither of us was in a position to cope with from a practical or emotional point of view. Thus followed a sad and lonely vigil to Victoria for us both to 'put things right' but the grief, the guilt and the sorrow was truly terrible.

Perhaps that is why I still feel that it is my responsibility that our subsequent marriage failed. Certainly my lack of confidence and esteem is why I felt no sense of outrage that he did not believe my stories of sexual abuse (instead demanding proof of them) and why I did not have the self-respect to question that he was not there to support me through these dreadful processes.

After all, clearly I didn't know what a proper relationship was, so it was 'all *MY* fault,' wasn't it?

It could not have been his...

Later in my life I am coming to realise that the above is the attitude of a victim, and a victim I no longer wish to be. So my boyfriend and I became husband and wife, sometime after I had purchased our home in his name in addition to my own. As he is the father of my beautiful and adorable daughter, my objective at this point is not to discredit his character – but simply to relay the story of my life and the effects my earlier abuse had on subsequent relationships.

I had issues with sexual intercourse during my marriage. Obviously due to earlier experiences of abuse, it was not a situation of ignorance of the activity – just a horror of it. What I craved for so desperately at this time in my early twenties (as ever) was love. Not sex, which I equated with exploitation and embarrassment – but love in the form of affection. Companionship, closeness and friendship were my desires but I had an ingrained belief system which dictated to me that I needed to express my love through sexual activities in order to please a man.

I must state that this situation for me improved in some ways throughout the union, but not enough...

We had a friendship and a sexual relationship but I spent much of my time feeling ostracised from my husband's singular passion for computer activities with his mates and my feelings of worthlessness were a paramount issue for me. All my life I had been made to feel unimportant and sadly my husband's carelessness in his attitude to me did nothing to alleviate this. I have strong recollections of my husband playing incessant video games with a mate and finding my presence to be an irritant. It is a vivid memory because this became an entrenched pattern in our life together. He would 'give' me money and suggest I go away and spend it at the casino, alone with the poker machines and out of his way.

My responsibility in this situation was that I did not have the self-respect or confidence to stand up for myself and demand better treatment, as many others would have done. I just wanted to spend time sharing things with him!

Predictably I guess, I developed an addiction to gambling. It is a common phenomenon that victims of abuse (sexual, psychological or emotional,) react to the world and its complications with self-defeating and sometimes destructive behaviours. Often sufferers of abuse go on to continue the cycle of abuse themselves, some self-harm or suicide, some become depressed and others go on to develop unhealthy dependencies on drugs, alcohol or sex. At this time in my life it was gambling that was my destructive force, coupled with the feelings of abandonment which accompanied the activity. I developed a friendship with a manipulative older man around this period, who encouraged me to leave my husband with his use of flattery and attention, which I was not getting at home. Suffice to say that for many reasons our marriage became untenable in the end.

Although now divorced, I will always have the entrenched joy that this relationship gave me my treasured little girl and the gift of motherhood. As parents together we have again become close friends, and I harbour no bad feelings towards the man I once married. At this point in my life (at around twenty-nine years of age,) I really had not yet come to terms with the fact that I was a survivor – I felt like a struggler without the appropriate tools to achieve the status of survivor.

Thus I made my next stupid decision.

I signed away all my rights to the house which I had been through so much hell to procure, as I was led to believe that by doing this our daughter would always have a home. It was a well-intentioned action on my part but is yet another example of how my past had ill-equipped me to stand up for myself or make intelligent decisions. Once again I had placed my future and myself into the hands of another rather than being independent and self-reliant and strong.

The ramifications of many unwise decisions such as this one are still causing me grief and financial difficulties in my life today and as with so much in my life I only wish that I could turn back time to make better choices.

Certainly I would have paid more attention to the advice given to me by my paid professional legal team on issues such as these.

THE END OF LOVE

Why am I so unhappy, lonely confused and sad? I do not have the words to use, except I always feel so bad.

You have been a friend to me, the father of my child but I am thrust away from you, a nuisance. I'm so wild!

My life's a tale of sorrow, betrayal, hurt and stealth.

And now you'd rather hang with mates than share with me, yourself.

I'm trying hard to sort my world and make a go of life.

But I need support and tenderness to play the role of wife.

Maybe we weren't meant to be.

How sad that is for us!

So I'll just leave, with one more wound, more reason not to trust.

Chapter Fourteen

A Mother Myself

How well I remember giving birth to my precious little baby daughter and the ferocious and protective wave of love which washed over me!

A brand new life, unsullied by the cruelty and the harshness of the world – all mine to love and protect as I was never loved or protected by my own mother. What perfection in her tiny features and her beautiful baby smell!

Here was my opportunity to right the horrendous wrongs of the past and to create an environment for *my* child that would be happy, positive, secure and content. As she now approaches womanhood with confidence and vigour and strength of character such as I have never known, I know that I have succeeded – despite me dealing still with my own past demons. In the writing of this book I needed to face one of them – am I really a good mother? I am certainly a diligent and protective one, but I find myself asking my daughter often if I love her enough – as I still do not know about love. To my delight and with the blessing of her father, Madelyn includes a page of her own in the book, describing in her own young words – her mother!

Chapter Fifteen

The Letter

Following is the verbatim transcript of the letter my daughter wrote and wished to be included as part of this book. Bless!

My Mum.

Hi everyone! If you are reading this, then you should know how hard my mother's life has been. My mother is human and nothing can change it.

My mother is everything to me aside from dad. At first I thought my life was bad but now after you read through my mum's story you'll understand how lucky I am to have her as a mum. She is the best mother ever. When she had me she said she didn't know how to treat me. Well she did know because here are my words telling you that she is just the best and most loving woman on earth. I love my mum dearly the same way I love my dad. I'm SO lucky to have a mother like Natasha Fay because she and dad spawned the best and only child they will ever have. Me! So thank you for understanding, and mum I love you.

xxxxxooooxxxoo. Madelyn

Chapter Sixteen

Spinning Out

Outwardly I appeared to be coping with my life after marriage. I worked hard, cared for my child and enjoyed my private time going out to places and venues where I felt safe and known. This period of my life however, was fraught with its own set of dangers and I was susceptible to very many of them due to my past abuse. Apart from gambling I enjoyed the relief from stress provided by drinking too many beers and thus appearing to be more confident and interesting than I could be in a sober state, and this led to other problems and various complications with men. By now I was entrenched in an unhealthy relationship with the older man whom I had met towards the end of my marriage. He was a real predator and had recognised me from the start as *"damaged goods"* he could use for his own purposes. Following this horrible episode, I went through a period of psychological reversal whereupon I wanted to be the user. *Me!* I tried to experience the power of using men for my own sexual purposes with no thought to their feelings or needs. This is a period of my life of which I am certainly not very proud. I include these admissions in my book to be honest and to help people to understand me, and hopefully understand themselves if they have walked in similar shoes. I just tried not to care. Fool that I was – I was continuing to hurt only myself because I still did not have the emotional tools with which to protect myself and move forward, to the extent that I repeated a horrific time of acute earlier grief and had to suffer through the guilt and anguish of another termination. Sex was obviously the reason the men I mixed with were interested in me and I certainly still had little enough self-respect to accommodate them in some warped predilections on that score, for a long time. It was a horrible period when I traded past abuse for self-abuse, in a way. These memories make me cringe, but all I can think of to justify my actions is that this episode of my life was actually a part of my journey towards self-discovery and healing and therefore necessary in an odd and uncomfortable way. I have decided to spare you the nasty details of these associations, suffice to say that I was merrily spinning on a downward spiral of gambling, alcohol and horrible sexual behaviour for a long time prior to me taking stock of myself and reversing the trend again, totally unsupported and alone.

They say a person has to reach 'rock bottom' before they can manage to take account of their life and their actions.

"They" don't know shit.

This saying appears to be the lip-service of judgemental people who feel superior to the rest of us who have human fallibilities of our own making or of the making of others. Somehow, I managed to draw back before I reached the abyss but I was lucky in that I had my beloved daughter to live a good and wholesome life for. Thus far in my period of spinning out following the marriage there had been no effect on her or her well-being, particularly as her father was present for her and shared the responsibility. I knew in my heart that there was no way she would suffer as I had done whilst I had breath in my body! I had a greater mission than myself to consider – that precious life to which I had given birth deserved all my love, my diligence and my care. I also knew that the juggling act of being a devoted mother and a 'mess' just could not be maintained as she grew older – something would have to give. I could not afford that to be her quality of care, or my health or sanity as her mother, as I was absolutely determined that her life and childhood would not be a reflection of my own. I wanted better for Madelyn than I had ever known or experienced for myself – security, love, support, protection, and a childhood free of fear and self-doubt. The journey has not been an easy one by any means but once again I overcame adversity alone, on her behalf, and have never looked back since.

Chapter Seventeen

Now – and Beyond

So here I am before you, in all my imperfections and with all my past horrors of sexual and other abuse exposed. I wonder what you think...

You must not think that I am a drama queen – that is the very last thing that I am.

I have found my story difficult to relate because it does not make me proud, or feel important. It is actually the polar opposite. I am terrified that by laying myself on the line I will further expose myself to abuse, of a social and personal kind. Maybe it will even affect my precious career which I love so much.

So be it. My story *needs* to be told.

I am not even sure when my status as an abuse victim changed to being that of survivor. I attended a positive thinking course prior to starting my career as a real estate agent which has helped me, and also spoke to a mental health nurse, who has been the ONLY person to ever ask about my past abuse. I will never forget her words – "I hear a lot of abuse stories but yours is one of the worst I have ever heard." Her empathy was amazing!

I had always convinced myself to believe that my life was not unusual, probably in order to cope with the horror. This wonderful lady allowed me to really comprehend that terrible crimes had been perpetrated against me and that I am a survivor. What a revelation this was!

I began to attend trauma counselling, which has helped me enormously. I feel so very much more positive about my life these days, I think I have developed the tools finally to deal with my past sexual exploitation and all the years of combined abuse I suffered. It is a very long road; this journey a tenuous one.

I am okay. Still lacking confidence, still lacking a man's proper love in my life but okay!

I have severed contacts with my past, with my mother and now rarely see my siblings. I need to do this in order to move forward.

Something I find hard to understand in this context is that I have a great curiosity concerning my biological father whom I have never met and feel a degree of responsibility towards him too, in the writing of this book.

I know through my mother, who he is and where he lives and have written to him (via registered post – so I know it has been received) informing him of my autobiography. I wish to cause him no grief and do not want anything from him – it just seems the appropriate thing to do.

When my mother last informed me that she was coming back to Tasmania for a visit, I responded relatively sternly that I would not see her.

I have taken enormous steps to eradicate any form of abuse in my life and whilst I know that for me the cycle is well and truly broken, the same cannot be said of her. Sad perhaps, but there it is. I have a duty to protect my daughter from all harm and as many negative influences as I can and for myself I want peace and privacy.

My siblings continue on in their respective lives and circumstances.

I care about them but I am on my own.

To my abusers;

I HOPE THAT YOU ROT IN HELL.

What I have decided to include at the very end stage of my story are the original police reports given to Tasmania Police regarding episodes of sexual abuse I have suffered. Obviously reports such as these by their nature have to be somewhat graphic and clinical which is why they were not included in the chronology of my life within the previous pages. But I have bared my soul to you and choose to hold nothing back. If they have any value to the reader it is to shock us all into becoming very much more vigilant in the protection of young people in our society whoever they are – a relative, a child in school, a church or youth group member, someone on a sports team, someone on a bus.

Abuse happens to children anywhere, everywhere and at any time, and we all have to be watchful and engaged to seek it out and stop it from happening.

I wish someone had noticed me… What a life I have had! All I know is that my heart really does bleed for all the other children of either sex, who have been trying to survive the journey of life such as I have endured.

My message to you is to bloody well stay alive!

While there is life there is hope. Do not ever take the blessed, easy way out – no matter who fails to notice your plight or support you, no matter how bereft you may feel. There really *IS* a light at the end of that very dark tunnel – even if that light has to come from within you.

The light, the future is your hands as it was in mine, but it is yours for the taking. Grab onto it, and determine that in your future you will cease to be a victim and become a survivor. *That is how you can beat them*, and have the happy and contented life that you deserve.

CORRESPONDENCE WITH MY MOTHER

(Sent via computer – Received)

Hello.

I understand you're coming to Tasmania in a couple of weeks. Please don't visit me. You told me to get over my past, well I'm doing that and I've had to deal with a lot, including the realisation that the abuse I suffered for many years by both (names removed) was bad but the abuse I suffered by you, my mother, was worse. Your constant put-downs and telling me you deliberately fell downstairs when pregnant to get rid of me, telling me I was a mistake and no good, forgetting about me at Christmas, my not knowing who my father was, you still didn't care. Putting us in and out of Swan House! You didn't want me so you should've left me there because I was happy there. There's so much more.

Don't show up at my house and don't show up at my work because you won't be seeing me at either. Also saying you feel sorry for Madelyn having a mum like me, well she is ALWAYS protected and I do have you to thank for this, because you showed me how NOT to treat my child. I may protect her too much but at least she is safe and we are close so she can and will always tell me anything which is how a relationship with a mother and daughter should be. You don't need to feel sorry for her, you need to feel sorry for yourself.

Natasha Fay.

LETTER TO MY FATHER
(Sent via Registered Post – Received no reply)

Hi (name removed.)

My name is Natasha and apparently you knew my mother (name removed) many, many years ago and in particular (apparently) as I am led to believe, the night I was conceived. I know you are not interested in finding out for sure if you're my dad, and that's not what this is about.

The reason for me writing is because I'm writing a biography and of course my shit life begins the night I was conceived, and yours is the only name mum has ever given me. I grew up with every form of abuse imaginable and now I don't have mum in my life (my choice.) I'm ready to deal with it and look towards a positive future.

I am a good person and I'm not writing my book for any reason except to help my own healing and hopefully help others who have been through similar. There are no names mentioned in my book and no-one will ever know about you.

My editor says I'm one of the strongest people she's ever met and my story is truly amazing and inspirational in so many ways. I don't see that and every time I read what's written I get teary and so does she, and she reckons everyone who reads it will have the same reaction.

Time will tell.

Anyway that's all I wanted to say.

Natasha.

The journey of my life and that of my daughter will continue, as we come to understand the meaning and purpose for being alive. For me it is she for whom I live and strive. The writing of this book was in itself a journey, as I have not only remembered and relived my past, but have discovered much new information in doing so (a lot of which it may take a long time for me to assimilate and absorb.) Due to my difficult relationship with my own mother, I turned to the Freedom of Information Act in order to fill in the many gaps and inconsistencies of the facts of my own childhood. This has been a revelation to me.

I had already learned that my mother changed our surname by deed poll when I was a child, which made the access of information somewhat more difficult. It was hard for me to realise that with the gathering of new information I needed the full support of my trauma counsellor once again as feelings of outrage, anger, disgust and sadness enveloped me at unexpected times.

I am still that confused little girl, but now with adult emotions which I can attach to her injustices and therefore can feel all the blocked out pain of a lifetime. I choose to see this as an unexpected and positive device in my healing, but it has been very difficult for me to face and overcome.

Excerpts from my Letter to the FOI Commissioner (2015)

"...requesting FOI documents... I am writing an autobiography. My childhood was 'rather bad' and... years of abuse and neglect from mother, and about 8 years of sexual abuse by (names removed.) ... in and out of Swan House which I believed was a respite place if parents couldn't cope.

I first sought info on Swan House (photos etc.) as this was my happy time as a child. It was a very important part of my childhood and it's a real shame I had to be taken from safety and put back into a nightmare. Since...I discovered it was run by Children's Protection Society ...I received information... but there was... a lot... blocked out.

My book... will help many people who come from similar backgrounds, and hopefully they can break the cycle of abuse, as I have done. My... abuse started the night I was conceived and I was often reminded of this. The rest of the abuse was extreme and regular and I need the blank spaces filled in.

As an adult, I struggle every day with what happened to me, but I have a good career and don't use my past as an excuse for the world to feel sorry for me... I'm hoping to make a difference...hopefully other victims will come forward as I did try the legal system with the men who sexually abused me but that came to no avail.

Please review the decision and allow me to have missing pages..."

Natasha Fay.

This letter was penned in response to an earlier reply I had received from FOI, explaining why information was removed from 'my family files'.

I quote an excerpt from this reply –

"Your situation is a little unusual in that an individual file for each of the children in your family was not created and everyone's information was combined into one file..." (Feb 2015.)

I honestly understand the rights of persons to their own privacy, but find it appalling that I have been denied information about my life because of *INCOMPETENT REPORTING!* I ended up receiving – from a total of 132 pages, 94 pages in full, 25 pages in part and 13 pages denied in full. I will continue to request reviews but it is hard for me not to assume that this is just another careless mistake made by a system which had direct influence over my life and which didn't care. Moving on, the information which I did actually receive shocked me more than I could have imagined. It was presented as a paper file with black ink blocking out that which I cannot read about myself. Some pages are missing. It emanates from the Dept. of Welfare Services, and is presented as case files on myself and my family from June 1979 to September 1985.

It consists mostly of reports from family aid workers, applications for family aide help (financial), meeting notes and dates of closing and re-opening of the file. Although the stated reason for intervention was, *"the well-being of the children"* and *"family stability"* it seems obvious that the focus was on neglect as there is no reference to sexual abuse in the records as such (unless blacked out.) Many references are made about budgeting and money, power and other services being withdrawn from the home, lack of a fridge and things of that nature. In October 1979, the Department received a report from our current school that we children were *"not adequately fed."* The response by the Department was to decide to make an appointment to visit my mother (she was already well known to them) and, *"try to stimulate a discussion about food provision for the children."*

I well remember those dreadful days of hunger, and can't help feeling that this response lacked proactivity and urgency. In 1980 my mother was given a monetary grant for *"accommodation for mother's break from family for 5 days."* The reason given was to avoid family breakdown. She wanted to put us in a "home" so she could focus on her own problems with her boyfriend, the report states.

In a report given to the Department by Children's Protection Society (staff at Swan House) it outlines that prior to our fourth admission there in June 1980, they considered that *"these children were surviving,"* however there was now a deterioration in the situation. Of me they said I was showing signs of emotional deprivation, I was demanding and craving of attention... had no deep emotional relationship with my mother, and so on. It states that I – *"have not asked for the mother, but seem relieved to be here."*

The report concludes thus -

"Because their family life is so disrupted I consider that all agencies concerned should consider the long term needs of the children. They must be provided with the opportunity, either as a group, or as individuals, to relate deeply with a warm and constant care person..."

Up to this point the revelations in writing about my general home life reflected my own memories, but still had the power to ignite alien emotions in me, namely fluctuating grief and red hot fury – emotions which I have never before allowed myself to feel. What happened next I have no memory of at all, so shock is now added to the mix...

In the same year and month of the above report I found a letter addressed to the Morwell Community Health Centre written by a qualified doctor, for tabling at a case conference on my family. It reads as follows –

"Called to house by police who said mother (name withheld) had tried to set fire to house and to kill herself and one daughter. At the house mother (name withheld) said she was very upset because (boyfriend) had apparently left town without warning. She admitted that she had tried to slash her wrists and had planned to kill her daughter. She said she had started the fire in the house but had not intended for it to get out of control.

In my opinion, she was not in fact suicidal, but in fact reacting as she has so often done, in an immature way to obtain sympathy and help from others. In this case however, her actions were so potentially dangerous to her children and to the property of others that there are grounds for having her children fostered long term. When discussing this with her that day she stated that if the children went to Swan House she would 'shoot through.'"

Signed by Dr (name removed) and dated 9/6/80.

Well! I *knew* I wasn't ever wanted...With my mind reeling, I continued reading all the material I had been sent wondering why on earth I have no memory of being rescued from the hideous existence at home, or of being fostered. Now I know, – NOTHING HAPPENED!

In a joint discussion the following day at the Morwell Shire Offices between parties and services involved with my family, it was agreed that up until then the person who had been predominately supporting my mother (name withheld) had been *"concerned about the general welfare of the children, whether they were adequately fed, the mother's priorities, and the mother's fluctuating behaviour – but had not considered the children to be 'at risk.'"*

It transpired that the doctor concerned was now prepared to support a Care and Protection Application, if welfare persons involved agreed. It was discussed that if this action was taken, it would allow the Children's Court to either – 1) Adjourn, to enable a detailed report to be furnished and children remain at Swan House on a Place of Safety Order during the interim period – 2) Demand a Supervision Order, 3) Decide on Wardship for all or specific children. 4) Adjourn on the condition that the mother be of good behaviour.

The outcome of this meeting seemed to reflect differing views, except for the consensus that mother (name withheld) be warned about the potential of a Care and Protection Order if she *"removes her children from Swan House before her doctor and other welfare persons feel she is ready to cope adequately with family matters again."*

By June 12th, the police had decided to take no action, but to review the situation in one month's time. By June 20th, a mere eleven days after the house fire, attempted suicide and threat to murder her daughter, also an assault on her ex-boyfriend, my mother had her children back at home under her care and protection – according to a home visit report written and dated by a welfare worker!

Honestly, I am forced to think that once again I was totally abandoned when I (and my siblings) most needed help. The family case file was closed in November of that year, 1980. I was a mere child of seven years old at that time, and as you already know, was a constant victim of sexual abuse which continued into my teens. This was obviously not known by the Welfare Department, but just how much more evidence was needed than what they already had to remove me from the situation I was forced to live in? It beggars belief.

Leafing back through the information, it seems the family moved on again, but remained in the system until at least the end of 1985, when I was twelve years old. In 1981 my mother went to Tasmania and we were left in the care of her partner (name withheld.) During that period, he became the subject of police involvement for *"leaving the children unattended"* and we went again to Swan House.

In Moe, in January 1984, a welfare worker on a home visit assigned *ONE* line in her report to the fact that my mother *"last night tried to commit suicide. (Name withheld) stopped her."*

One line... During that very same month – in an application for family aide help – the woman writes that *"Mother has trouble coping with children, has bashed them in the past...Mum (name withheld) suffers from depression. Also has bad temper and has hit children... feels trapped in house – needs to get out more..."* The following month a family aid worker writes, *"Discussed the problems that (name withheld) is experiencing, these being her temper with her children... fear of bashing her children... problems with coping with her nerves. Difficulties in disciplining and communicating with her children..."*

Obviously this and other well-meaning workers tried to help my mother by formulating goals, budgets, listening to her and writing reports – but where did the children's welfare and safety factor in to all this? I really have to wonder.

One report I found fascinating consisted of these words (as the result of a home visit) – *"Mother (name withheld) has been coping well as she now has contact with a couple more males and therefore has had some cash to buy clothes for the children."* June 1984. August 1984 – *"Mother (name withheld) is confused as to her future. This takes priority over the children's welfare..."*

September 1984 – *"...It is doubtful as to whether much more can be accomplished in this family by a family aide/family counsellor, the basic goals set when F/A began involvement have been reached and this family presents as being one that goes from crisis to crisis."*

The outcome of this report is that services were withdrawn. How can the goals of the well-being of the children and family stability have possibly been reached, when the report writer freely admitted that my family went (and would continue to go,) from crisis to crisis?

Probably they were all good and caring individuals, but something is certainly not right about it all. Maybe they did all within their power to help us, but I am living testimony that it was not enough. It is not my wish to douse the reader with copious reports, but I have always maintained that my abuse went even beyond the horrific sexual crimes perpetrated against me and I want to be understood, for the sake of others and for my own integrity.

I also wonder about the professionalism of some who were assigned to our case... In January 1985, when services were reinstated, an excerpt from a home visit by a family aid worker reads -

"I must admit I find the mother (name withheld) a little hard to take at times but I guess somewhere down there a person is struggling to get out..."

"Mother (name withheld) is 'ok.' – Still 'fumbling' along!"- March 15th, 1985. This sentence constitutes the ENTIRE home visit report which occurred on that particular day!

And on it goes – *"Things ok on last visit."* June 21st, 1985.

"Things seem ok with mum." July 5th, 1985.

"Things seem ok with mum." August 18th, 1985.

These comments are not "typos," but rather a repetitive sentence used to report back on specifically identified problems of my mother's handling of her children, amongst other issues specified by the Department as areas of need within the family.

I am amazed and incredibly saddened that we, as children, mattered so very little.

Family aide was once again withdrawn when mum decided to move us back to Tasmania, although she availed herself of services there when we arrived. Naturally, it has to be explained that I have chosen only relevant passages from those FOI files which relate (in the main) to me, in order to protect the identities of others. Some may seem to be taken out of context, but I would strongly disagree, as I have been overlooked for *far too long!*

It is the condition of my life and the horrors that befell me that are the direct subject of my book, and how I managed to overcome adversity on so very many levels. This is one level that has shocked me in the present day, as I now realize that yet another system has let me down dreadfully.

As the true story of my life to date concludes, I am feeling so much more centred and strong. I can cry for the little damaged, abused, unloved and unwanted child that I was, and have allowed many of my emotions to rise to the surface.

For me it has been very important to include reports from police, doctors, courts and all the other agencies involved because I still now, as an adult, am scared that I may not be believed. I guess that is part of my recovery process – to understand that I am worthy of the caring and validation of others.

I am left, after this process, with some searing and important questions which I would like to share with you, as you have cared enough to share my journey. In no particular order, these are the issues which continue to keep me awake long into the night. Why, why, why did my treating doctors not report my neglect as a child? They knew the family well (even reported on the fire and the fact that my mother tried to kill us,) and why did staff in the various schools I attended do little more than send a report to welfare that we were always hungry? I guess the question is somewhat rhetorical in a way, because if they cared enough or were observant enough, this would surely have happened.

It does break my heart though, for it could have spared me years of agony at the hands of my neglectful mother and my other sexual abusers.

In the letter sent by the Office of Director of Public Prosecution (dated 20th September 1994 and included in the book) to the Legal Aid Commission, it clearly states that a sister of mine had said in an interview that she had also been raped by the same two men as me. It also states that she would not give evidence. *How can that be?* If there was corroboration that my sexual abuse and rape had occurred (and there obviously was!) how could the legal system *decide not to prosecute* the men? Surely my sister would have told the truth in a court situation, even if she had to be subpoenaed!

Why on earth was the whole thing not important enough to follow up? I understand that if you see or experience a crime this evil, you can be instructed to tell about it, for the reason of justice and to uphold the law. I bear no grudge for my sister, but I certainly feel that the legal system was in the wrong in this instance and failed in its duty of care to me.

Also in this letter, (the final sentence) – *"Your client has stated that she reported sexual assault to her supervisor at (name removed) High. That lady recalls no such report."*

However, SASS, in their report to the Criminal Injuries Compensation Court, state quite plainly that -

"Natasha first contacted the service in 1/11/89. She was referred by her school guidance officer who accompanied her."

They asked the *WRONG* woman!

My other sister was not interviewed *at all!* I ask again, why? If my mother was telling me the truth about being interviewed by police and stating that she -

"...knew something was going on, but didn't know what to do about it"- regarding my sexual abuse, one would reasonably assume that the police should have acted upon her statement alone...

In the letter from my Tasmanian lawyers (included in the book) it states clearly that, *"Mrs. (name removed, lawyer) was appalled at the non-attention your matter attracted from the Victorian police... the police have not seen fit to even interview the offenders..."*

It appears once again that the law system failed in its duty of care to me, this time in Victoria.

In the latter part of my story it is obvious that the Department of Welfare Services were remiss in their duty of care as well, starting from the fact that "*an individual file...*" was not even created for me, which was "*unusual.*" As you have read, the litany of woeful interactions between this department and my family covered several years, and they chose not to act upon the report from Swan House, nor did they act after my mother tried to burn down the house and kill her daughter. We were returned to her care within *ELEVEN DAYS!* I find this situation preposterous in the extreme, and am very disturbed by the unprofessional home visit reports and the fact that services were withdrawn as, "*...This family appears as being one that goes from crisis to crisis.*" Somehow I am also bothered by the fact that I never knew (until researching for this book) that I was constantly staying in child protection homes and was a part of the welfare system for so many years – a mighty shock!

Ah, you may say, it's all in the past now, and I guess it is. Would that I could turn back time and see all these questions answered and mistakes corrected! But in a way, it is my present as well, as I continue to deal with the ramifications of abuse, neglect and the systems which failed in their duty of care for me.

And it will all live on into my future...

Thank you for listening. My earnest hope is that by baring my life and experiences with you, we will together stand up and be counted – watch for signs of abuse and neglect of children everywhere, and should you know a sexual predator do not look away. Take your suspicions to the police. It may save another life.

If you are a victim of abuse, I am here as a living testimony to show you that – even with all the odds stacked up against at every turn – you too can find the strength from within to become a survivor.

A PLEA – FROM THE HEART

If you were to walk a mile in my shoes, you'd understand so many things, enough about life to give you the blues, at the pain that child abuse brings.

Having no-one to turn to, no-one to trust, leaves a legacy of fear and of pain. Put my sad story away if you must, but please stop it from happening again!

Don't show me pity, show me your courage, to learn from my story of grief and muster up a true sense of outrage, to provide other poor victims relief.

It is never their fault, though they get the blame on one level or on another,

From friends and from family and services that shame and at times – just like me – from their mother.

Look out for the quiet one, a child with no smile and find out what is going on

Get involved and let's walk that one extra mile, 'til the crime of abusing a child is far gone.

TASMANIA POLICE

OFFICE OF ORIGIN:

Inspector's Office
Hobart C.I.B.
Capita Building
Cnr. Argyle and
  Liverpool Streets
HOBART TAS 7000

9 October 1992

Mr. ▮
Legal Aid Commission
 of Tasmania
123 Collins Street
HOBART TAS 7000

Dear Sir

Re: Natasha Fay ▮

I refer to your letter dated 23rd September 1992.

Enclosed are four statements of Natasha ▮:

25th January 1992, prepared by Miss ▮
29th January 1992, taken by Constable ▮
4th February 1992, taken by Constable ▮
28th February 1992, taken by Constable ▮

Yours faithfully

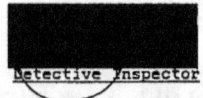

Detective Inspector

P.D. No. 109

TASMANIA  POLICE

5.30pm

STATEMENT Date 29 January 1992

Name of Witness	▓▓▓	Natasha Fay
	Surname (in capitals)	Christian Names
Address	▓▓▓	Age D.O.B. 13.11.73
Occupation	Receptionist/Typist	Phone ▓▓▓
Name and Address of Employer	▓▓▓	
	Sandy Bay	Phone ▓▓▓

My full name is Natasha Fay ▓▓▓. I was born in Hobart in 1973.

On 21st January 1992, I wrote a letter to the Police Department because I have decided that I want something done about the sexual abuse that I suffered as a child.

Over the weekend of the 25/26 and 27 January, I wrote down what I can remember about what happened.

In 1975, we moved to Melbourne when mum and her husband divorced. My mother is ▓▓▓ (4.3.50) - she now lives in Forster Street, New Town. As far as I know, her husband was my father. His name is ▓▓▓ (about 44 y.o.), he lives in ▓▓▓ Goulburn Street, Hobart. When we moved there was my half brother, ▓▓▓ (21 years old) and half sister ▓▓▓ ▓▓▓ (19 years), my mother and me.

I can't remember when my mother moved in with ▓▓▓, I was too young to remember. While we were there, we lived in Melbourne, Sale, Morwell, Erica, Newborough, Traralgon, Moe - where we stayed until we moved back to Tasmania. I went to primary school in Morwell prep to gd. 2; Erica Rural School ¹ gd. 3; Newborough gd. 3; Primary Traralgon Primary - beginning gd. 4; Elizabeth Street Primary in Moe - gd. 4 - gd. 6. We moved to Tasmania in October 1984 and I went to Princes Street Primary School in Sandy Bay. My younger sister ▓▓▓, was born in Melbourne in 1976. Her father was killed in a car accident.

▓▓▓, ▓▓▓ (his middle name might be ▓▓▓). He's about 21 years old now. He was also living with us in Victoria. It was never a happy household.

P.D. 109A

STATEMENT — *Continued*

Name of Witness		Natasha Fay
	Surname (in capitals)	Christian Names

▓▓▓▓ was working with the S.E.C. all the time we were there. He now runs a 2nd hand shop in ▓▓▓▓

I was sexually abused by ▓▓▓▓ from when I was 5 years old until we left when I was 11 y.o. I know that he also abused my sister, ▓▓▓. She told me this about 2 years ago. I asked her if she wanted to say anything to support me. She said, "No, I don't want anything to do with it." I don't know if he abused ▓▓▓▓ - when I asked her she said she was too young to remember.

▓▓▓▓ (age 21) and ▓▓▓▓ (age 20) ▓▓▓▓ were friends of ▓▓▓'s - they were all in the marching team together. Whenever the team went away for competitions, ▓▓▓▓ would take all the girls to the competition. He used to insist on ▓▓▓▓ and ▓▓▓▓ staying over. My mother went to Melbourne in June 1990, and she said that she spoke to ▓▓▓▓ and they told her they had been abused by ▓▓▓▓ and wanted to prosecute. I know that they live in Churchill in Melbourne. The marching team was called "▓▓▓▓'s Marching Team". That was about 1980-81.

I was also abused by ▓▓▓▓. He was a family friend. I believe he's living in the house he owns in Yallourn North. He was married and had two children - I think they are boys. I heard that he and his wife had split up after he put one of the children in hospital. I don't think he was working and he used to hang out at the local TAB. I think he'd be about 44 years old now. As far as I know he has not abused ▓▓▓ or anyone else in my family.

All the abuse except for three incidents occurred in Victoria.

These incidents happened in Hobart. It would have been in February or March when I was in grade 7 at ▓▓▓▓ - that would have been in 1986. ▓▓▓▓ broke his ankle and came over to Tasmania to stay with my mother for two weeks. We were living with my uncle at ▓▓▓▓, Sandy Bay. (My uncle is ▓▓▓▓). I remember that it happened on a Wednesday, a Thursday, a Saturday - I'm not sure why I remember those days. The first time I was in the lounge room - it would have been about 9 in the morning. Mum told me that ▓▓▓▓ wanted his back scratched and she told me to go to her bedroom where he was. I was scared because I thought it would happen - that's how it always started with ▓▓▓▓ asking to to have his back scratched. I went to her bedroom and she got in the bed as well. I was inside the bed between ▓▓▓▓ and mum. I scratched his back like he wanted then mum hopped out and went to have a shower

Name of Witness		Natasha Fay
	Surname (in capitals)	Christian Names

leaving me in the bed with ▇▇▇. Once she was out of the room, he rolled over and started moving his hands over my body and down. I can't remember what I was wearing, but I was clothed. He took my clothes off from the waist down then he rolled on top of me. He touched me and put his fingers inside me then he put his penis inside my vagina. He didn't stay there long, he just stopped and rolled off. I jumped out of the bed. He didn't say anything or threaten me. I didn't say anything either. I went along with him because it had happened for so long. I didn't think I had an option but to go along with him.

The other two times happened in the same bed, but my mother had nothing to do with those.

▇▇▇ started touching me all over my body when I was 5 years old. He would touch me under my clothes over my stomach and chest area. I can't remember if he touched me in the area of my vagina. I remember feeling that it wasn't supposed to happen. I cannot remember the first time he touched me like that.

The first abuse that I remember clearly was by ▇▇▇ at Traralgon Show in November 1978. I have described this on page 2 of my statement. ▇▇▇ had touched me under my clothes in a similar way to ▇▇▇ before this time. I cannot remember if he touched me in the area of my vagina.

He didn't give me the money he promised me. That was the only occasion he promised money. When we stayed at ▇▇▇'s that was a house in Morwell. I think he was renting the house.

The first time ▇▇▇ had full sexual intercourse with me would have been when I was 6 years old. I cannot remember it specifically because the touching just got more – more until it became full sexual intercourse. He would have intercourse with me about once a week except when he and mum had a fight. When that happened he would leave for a few weeks.

It usually happened in the bedroom ▇▇▇ shared with mum. It always started with ▇▇▇ asking me to scratch his back. When he'd had enough of that he would roll over and start touching my body under my clothes. He would take my clothes off from the waist down then hop on top. I was always on my back. He never asked me to do anything to him. Before he started having full intercourse with me he used to put his penis in my mouth, but that stopped. He can't remember if he said anything during it. I don't remember him telling me not to tell

P.D. 109A

STATEMENT — *Continued*

Name of Witness	▓▓▓▓▓▓	Natasha Fay
	Surname (in capitals)	Christian Names

anyone. I was scared of him, but I don't know what I thought he'd do. He wasn't violent. I often thought about telling my mother but I always thought she'd blame me, we've never got on and she always told me I was a mistake.

I never liked ▓▓▓▓, I don't know what my brother and sisters thought of him.

The only incident I remember clearly with ▓▓▓▓ was the one I described on page 1 of my statement, when I went back to Victoria for the September holidays in 1986. It only happened the first night I stayed with him and that's the last time he did anything to me. It was also the first time I protested in any way - although I was still too scared to open my mouth and say anything. When I said that he hopped on top of me - he went on and had intercourse with me.

I first got my periods in Grade 7. ▓▓▓▓ never said anything about contraception. I don't know if he was circumcised or not.

I don't remember how often ▓▓▓▓▓▓ abused me. Our family used to visit when they lived in Yallourn N. We probably visited a couple of times a month. It didn't happen every time we went to visit. When it did, it was either in the lounge room or in his bedroom.

We would usually stay overnight and the abuse always happened at night. One time I remember - I think I was 6 or 7 years old - I was sleeping in the lounge. He came out and asked me if I wanted to sleep with him and his wife. I said "Yes" because I thought nothing would happen if his wife was there. I was on one side, he was in the middle and his wife was on the far side. He touched me all over my body, under my clothes. He put his hand inside my knickers and put his finger inside my vagina. I turned away and he stopped.

He sometimes had intercourse with me. When his wife was out (sometimes she went to the pub or out visiting) it would happen in his bedroom. It was the same as with ▓▓▓▓ I didn't think I had an option because I was too young.

In 1989, when I was in grade 10, I was kicked out of home by my mother. I went to see the grade 10 Supervisor at ▓▓▓▓▓▓▓▓▓▓▓▓. I told her about the sexual abuse because I thought it was about time I told someone about it. ▓▓▓▓ took me to see the school social worker (I can't remember her name) to see about accommodation and getting the Young Homeless Allowance. I also told

STATEMENT — *Continued*

Name of Witness	███████	Natasha Fay
	Surname (in capitals)	Christian Names

her about the abuse and she organised for me to go to S.A.S.S. I only went once, I didn't feel I was ready to go through it all in detail.

I am now in a stable relationship with ███████. It's because of this that I have decided that I want something done about the abuse I have suffered over the years.

N. ███████

P.D. No. 109

TASMANIA  POLICE

STATEMENT Date 28.2.92

Name of Witness	Surname (in capitals)	Natasha Christian Names	
Address		Age D.O.B.	13.11.73
Occupation	Receptionist/Typist	Phone	
Name and Address of Employer	Legal Practice Sandy Bay	Phone	

In my first statement I said that we moved back to Hobart in October 1984. I remember now that I started school at Princes Street, Sandy Bay in October 1985 - I was in grade 6. So we arrived back in Hobart in October 1985. ▇▇▇ came over soon after that and stayed with us over Christmas and New Year 1985/86 at ▇▇▇▇▇▇▇▇▇▇, Sandy Bay. That's when the three incidents I put in my first statement happened.

The incident I described when I went to Victoria in Grade 7 (1986). The school holidays are usually about the first two weeks in September. ▇▇▇ was living at ▇▇▇▇▇▇▇▇, Marwell then, that's where it happened.

I spoke to the counsellor I'm seeing at S.A.S.S. and told her it was okay to tell Constable ▇▇▇ when I went to see them in 1989.

I cannot remember if we met ▇▇▇▇▇▇ before or after ▇▇▇▇ moved in with us. I know the Traralgon Show is in November but I cannot remember if it was 1978 or 1979 when ▇▇▇▇ took me there. My mother definitely took me to the doctor after that so Dr ▇▇▇ should be able to say if it was November 78 or November 79.

N ▇▇▇▇

Statement taken by me at CIB office, 28 February.
▇▇▇▇
Const ▇▇

P.D. No. 109

TASMANIA  POLICE

STATEMENT

Date: 4 Feb 92

Name of Witness	Surname (in capitals)	Natasha. Christian Names
Address		Age D.O.B. 13.11.73
Occupation	Receptionist/Typist	Phone
Name and Address of Employer	Legal Practice	
		Phone

In the last week of October 1989, when I was in grade 10, I had taken ▓ encyclopaedias to school to study for exams. Mum asked me to bring one of them back for ▓ and I forgot. I forgot to bring it back that week. On the 1st November, when I still didn't have the encyclopaedia, she said "You can pack your bags and get out."

I packed my things and when mum was out, I phoned a friend, ▓, and she and her boyfriend came and picked me up.

When I went to Victoria in the September holidays 1986, the people I stayed with were ▓, Hernes Oak.

When ▓ abused me, it was not always full intercourse, sometimes it was playing with his hands around my body. On the statement I wrote myself, I said that this happened 1-5 times a fortnight - that was general abuse. He had intercourse with me about once a week - that's what I said in my second statement.

I started keeping a diary in 1988 - that's the one my mother read. I did talk about the next-door neighbour in it and I have talked about going to S.A.S.S. and Mrs. ▓. There wasn't much about ▓.

N. ▓

My name is Natasha Fay ▇▇▇. I am 18 years old, born 13/11/1973.

I am the daughter of ▇▇▇ and I have 2 sisters - ▇▇▇, 19 and ▇▇▇, 15 I also I have 1 brother, ▇▇▇.

When I was 5 years old I started being sexually abused by my stepfather, ▇▇▇ of Morwell, believed to be living with his mother, and an old friend of the family, ▇▇▇, believed still to live in Yallourn North somewhere.

I have been told to try and remember everything that happened, when, where, approximately what time, date, and place, but it is an impossible task to do.

It is very hard to remember what time and when it happened, etc, but I do know that to start off with they would only caress my body and play with me a little bit, although ▇▇▇ would put his penis in my mouth and start moving his body up and down.

There are some moments that I remember as if it only happened yesterday.

When I was about 6, ▇▇▇ would ask me to scratch his back, and being young I didn't think there would be anything wrong with that. Then he would roll over and move his hands over my body. He would then put his finger inside my vagina and then his penis.

I was frightened and I thought if I told someone they would think it was my fault, or if I didn't do as he said, he would tell someone, and I would get into trouble and not him.

This would happen mostly in the afternoon or morning before school. It happened about 1 - 5 times a fortnight, sometimes less, sometimes more, until my family moved over here.

I went back to Victoria in the September holidays in 1986, when I was in grade 7. I spent the first week at a friends place and stayed with ▇▇▇ the second week. ▇▇▇ complained because he took the first week off work so he could take me places.

The night I returned to his place he went into my bedroom and took me into his. He pushed me down the bed until my mouth was level with his penis and with his hands on the back of my head moved it up and down.

Then he pulled me off and went down and was licking my vagina. I closed my legs and tightened my vagina so he would stop, he told me to stop it and that he couldn't breath properly. He stopped after a little while and hopped on top of me.

▇▇▇ also did this to my sister ▇▇▇, but she doesn't want to do anything about it. Also believed to a ▇▇▇, as they were known then of Churchill, Victoria.

▓▓▓▓▓▓ was the guy who actually broke my virginity.

He and his wife took their two kids, my brother, and I to the Traralgon show in November of 1978, when I was 5 years old.

▓▓▓▓▓▓ got lost and so ▓▓▓▓▓▓ told his wife that we were going to go and look for him.

I knew what he was going to do, because both he and ▓▓▓▓▓▓ played around with me before that, but didn't actually break my virginity.

I was scared and didn't want to go, but he insisted.

He was taking me over toward the girls toilets, and wouldn't let me go. I got away from him and ran over to a stall of some sort, ▓▓▓▓▓▓ said something to the lady and she told me not to worry, and that there would be a parachute or something coming along soon.

▓▓▓▓▓▓ got hold of me again, and took me into the toilets. I guess no one thought it was weird because I was only 5. Anyway, he stood me up on the toilet seat and placed his knees on the seat to keep my legs from shutting.

He then pulled my knickers down, and stuck his finger inside my vagina, he pushed it up as far as it would go, and it hurt like nothing else. The tears were just pouring out of my eyes and I was so scared but there was nothing I could do.

When he decided he'd had enough, he pulled my knickers up, put me on the floor, grabbed my hand and left. I was in pain and I even had trouble walking, the tears were still very strong. When we got outside he told me that he would give me $50.00.

We found my brother, and ▓▓▓▓▓▓ told him that I also got lost, which was the reason why I was crying.

My brother and I stayed at ▓▓▓▓▓▓'s place that night, and I had a bath and I seen that my knickers were covered in blood, so I started crying again.

That night I had to sleep on the couch, I was scared and I wanted to sleep with my brother, but ▓▓▓▓▓▓ said that I wasn't allowed to, so I had to sleep on the lounge.

He came out into the lounge room that night and started moving his hands around my body, then his wife called out after him and he went into the kitchen to get a glass of water.

When I got home the next day, I tried hiding my knickers under some clothes in the laundry at home. It didn't do any good because mum found them, I told her they were my older sisters knickers, not mine, she didn't believe me, so then I said I had a blood nose.

She didn't believe that either, so she took me down to the doctors to get me checked out. I didn't know how she would react if I told her what happened. I thought she would've said it was all my fault. She kept telling me how much of a mistake I was and I was scared to even talk to her.

This, I believe has been the reason for me to become scared or frightened of men, especially older men. Even those who would be the most trustworthy men on this earth, when I get alone, (whether in a car etc) with them I go all scared and start thinking of what happened to me as a child.

www.ingramcontent.com/pod-product-compliance
Lightning Source LLC
Chambersburg PA
CBHW051951290426
44110CB00015B/2191